SOUTHWEST
VIRGINIA
—— AND ——
MARITIME
DISASTERS

SOUTHWEST VIRGINIA

VIRGINIA

— AND —

MARITIME DISASTERS

FROM THE SS *VESTRIS* TO THE *MORRO CASTLE*
AND BEYOND

BRANDON WHITED

THE
History
PRESS

Published by The History Press
Charleston, SC
www.historypress.com

Front cover: author's collection.
Back cover, top left: courtesy of Sam Crimm II; *center left*: Naval History and Heritage Command; *bottom left*: courtesy of Betsy Smith McLain; *right*: Naval History and Heritage Command.

First published 2024

Manufactured in the United States

ISBN 9781467155915

Library of Congress Control Number: 2023947100

I humbly dedicate this work to the region in which I have lived my entire life.

CONTENTS

FOREWORD

One lives in the hope of becoming a memory.
—Antonio Porchia

When a tragedy happens, it has the trickle effect of touching an entire area where there are local connections. Then, with each passing year, for generation after generation, these events and those involved slowly drift from consciousness.

It takes a determined researcher to scroll through faded microfilm, open dusty photo albums, make their way through old cemeteries and cross-reference family trees to find relatives of those involved in something historical.

Brandon Whited takes readers through his adventures in his fact-finding mission. That mission? To explore those from Southwest Virginia who were involved directly and indirectly in maritime disasters.

Sailing by ship is not like today, where it is done mostly to go on vacation; it was an important means of travel. The people in this book boarded their ships for myriad reasons. Brandon lays out a meticulous timeline of events of these denizens of the region that goes straight through to the tragedies.

The names of some of the ships, such as *Titanic* and *Lusitania*, are familiar to most people through school lessons, but people are often unaware of local ties to them. This new publication by Brandon will hopefully encourage others to learn more about these incidents or to pursue other local history. The Southwest Virginians who are the focus of this book have become a memory once again.

—Michael Poirier
Rhode Island
Coauthor, *Into the Danger Zone: Sea Crossings of the First World War*

ACKNOWLEDGEMENTS

No project of this nature could come together without the assistance and support of many individuals. Though it will be difficult to name them all, I will do my utmost to extend my appreciation.

My parents, Ralph and Phyllis Whited, have always been encouraging of my writing pursuits, from offering parental praise on finished pieces to letting me stage readings of my middle-school short stories in the living room. My wife, Julian, has been incredibly supportive of a husband who often spends his scant spare time hunched over a notebook or staring at a century-old newspaper archive on the computer screen.

My dear friends, especially Robert Vance and Lee and Renee Liguore, have always uplifted me during the often strenuous process of tackling a new writing project, and I am deeply grateful for them.

My wonderful friend Michael Poirier, a fellow trustee with Titanic International Society, years ago showed me the ropes and advised me on how to conduct my own original research. I am always grateful for Mike's advice and friendship, and I was honored to have him write the foreword to this book. Michael Beatty, also a fellow trustee in the society, provided insight into *The White Ghost of Disaster*, the early *Titanic* film that played throughout Southwest Virginia in 1914. Randy Bryan Bigham, a longtime friend and noted historian, also weighed in on the film and has always been helpful and encouraging of my work. Author and historian Tad Fitch was always willing to provide valuable publishing insights and advice. Charles Haas, president of Titanic International Society, has always been a proponent of my writing and research, and he published two of the stories contained herein in a shorter form in *Voyage*, the society's quarterly journal.

When conducting research on individuals who lived long ago, families are often a fount of knowledge that could never be acquired in an archive, and I was very fortunate to have the selfless assistance of several descendants while conducting my research for this book. Sam Crimm II, a cousin of Pearl Harbor victim Warren Harding Crim, went above and beyond, sending me scores of documents about Warren and openly sharing all the photographs and knowledge he held about his heroic cousin. Betsy Smith McLain, granddaughter of *Titanic* survivor Mary Eloise Hughes and victim Lucian Philip Smith, is a dear friend who has always supported my research into her family's tragic story. She allowed the use of the beautiful portrait of her grandmother seen in this book. Linda H. Daniel, daughter-in-law of *Titanic* survivor Robert Williams Daniel, allowed me the honor of being the first *Titanic* researcher to whom she ever spoke regarding her mysterious father-in-law's harrowing experience in 1912. I am indebted to her for the insights into Robert's character that her recollections provided. Marian Brune McCreary provided great information and photographs of her husband's uncle, Frank Elmer McCreary, who died in a Japanese POW camp in 1943 after surviving alongside Commander David Albert Hurt the scuttling of the USS *Perch*. Sandra Holt, granddaughter of *Morro Castle* victim Harry Acree Lipscomb, recalled at great length the stories she was told about her grandfather, providing a wonderful insight into the person he was. Harold Richardson, a son of Stuart Richardson, recounted for me what his father had told him about his voyage aboard the *Queen Mary* during World War II.

Worshipful Master Shane Bouton of King Lodge No. 461 diligently searched the Masonic lodge's records for mention of William J. Bachman and his family. Edgar A. Rice made available images and a brief biography of Daniel Ray Arrington, killed in the kamikaze attack on the USS *Bunker Hill*.

Kate Jenkins, my commissioning editor at The History Press, was phenomenal from the start in her support of bringing this project to its fruition. I am thankful for her assistance throughout, as well as for her quelling my anxiety at various stages of the publishing process!

Photographers Linsey McKnight and Kalyn Newberry both volunteered to be on standby in order to bail me out should I encounter any technical difficulties in taking or formatting the images that appear in this book. I am thankful to them for having my back.

Should I have neglected to mention anyone else who deserves to be listed here, please be assured that this was not intentional and that your support and assistance are greatly appreciated!

INTRODUCTION

S outhwest Virginia is a region with a storied past. In most instances, these stories have been told already. The area's legacy of coal mining, American Civil War battles and general southern folklore has been researched, analyzed and collected in numerous volumes over many years. More important, not only have these histories been collected, but they are also remembered. But there is one aspect of the region's rich history that has been glaringly omitted from our books and collective memories. I am speaking of Southwest Virginia's surprisingly dense maritime history.

The genesis of this project occurred in early 2017, when I read Clint Olivier's excellent book *Last Dance of the* Vestris, which recounts the 1928 sinking of the steamship *Vestris* off the coast of Virginia, resulting in the loss of 117 lives. As stated in the book, one of the first-class victims, Ernest Alonzo Jackson, was born in Glade Spring, Virginia. Further investigation revealed that when Ernest and his family were not occupied with their Baptist missionary work in Brazil, the Jacksons resided in Abingdon, Virginia. It was this intriguing revelation that inspired me to search for other links within our region to famous maritime disasters. And what a surprising number turned up! Originally conceived as a medium-sized article, my idea soon swelled into a book project.

Really, it only makes sense that Southwest Virginia would have some links to maritime history, for if anyone had need or desire to travel to Europe or South America before the middle of the twentieth century, they could only do so by steamship. As maritime historian John Maxtone-Graham put it succinctly, it was "the only way to cross." Therefore, the surprise lay not in the fact that the links exist but that, with very few exceptions, they have been almost completely forgotten. Returning to the example of the Jackson family from Abingdon, I visited that town's historical society in the spring of 2018 to conduct further research on the family and their loss on the *Vestris*. Inquiries about the 1928 disaster were met with blank looks. There was nothing in the society's extensive archives about Ernest Alonzo, Jannette or Cary Jackson, let alone their fateful voyage. As the sea had washed away their bodies, so, too, time had seemingly washed away the memories of them. It proved to be that the case of the Jacksons was not unique in this regard.

The purpose of this book is not to present a definitive list of all of Southwest Virginia's connections to maritime history. That herculean task is not fit for one person, as there undoubtedly are many other connections yet to come to light. Perhaps the publication of this book will bring some more of them to the surface (no pun intended). Rather, *Southwest Virginia and Maritime Disasters* is intended to present the stories of individuals from the region who were connected to some of the more prominent episodes in maritime history—RMS *Titanic*, Pearl Harbor, etc. As the narrative is focused on telling the stories of these individuals, seasoned researchers and maritime historians will likely find little new regarding the events themselves but will learn much about the events' forgotten participants who called Southwest Virginia home.

The majority of links detailed in this book are each given their own chapter, whereas a general chapter, "Doughboys and GIs," details the stories of a few of the many brave young men from our region who crossed the sea to serve our country during the epoch-making conflicts of World War I and World War II. Major wartime events, such as Pearl Harbor, are given their own chapter. The events are organized within the book chronologically. The final chapter, "Various Stories," relates tidbits of information that would not fit properly into any of the main chapters. The information presented in that chapter spans many decades and covers the entire region. As with the other chapters, these snippets are presented in chronological order.

It is my most sincere hope that this book might spark an interest in our region's links to maritime history. These individuals have, collectively, been forgotten for far too long. Should this humble work at least momentarily bring them to the forefront of the reader's mind, I will count the book a resounding success. Only by telling and retelling their stories can we prevent the names and faces of the people you are about to meet from being forever washed away by the tides of time.

1

SS COLUMBIA

WILLIAM J. BACHMAN

Though almost entirely forgotten today, in its own time, the SS *Columbia* was a floating wonder of technology. *Columbia* demonstrated a lighting system designed by and installed under the supervision of the legendary American inventor Thomas Edison. This was, in fact, the first use of his patented lighting system for commercial purposes outside his Menlo Park, New Jersey laboratory. The vessel had another first in maritime history: the installation of an electric dynamo.

At 334 feet in length, the *Columbia* successfully plied the route from Portland, Oregon, to San Francisco, California, for just over twenty-seven years, from its maiden voyage in June 1880 until its tragic sinking on July 21, 1907.

Among the eighty-eight people who lost their lives in the sinking of the *Columbia* was thirty-eight-year-old William J. Bachman of Bristol, Virginia. With the passage of nearly 115 years since his untimely death, biographical details for Bachman are scant, and only a single, poor-quality newspaper photograph is known to survive. But enough is known to paint a word-portrait of a hardworking, upstanding family man who was well thought of by those who knew him.

(The city of Bristol is bisected by the boundary line between Virginia and Tennessee; thus, certain locations referred to in this story took place on the Virginia side and others on the Tennessee side.)

Above: The SS *Columbia* is seen here in its glory days. *Wikimedia Commons.*

Opposite: William J. Bachman's voyage on the *Columbia* was part of a vacation rewarded him through his work as an insurance salesman. *Author's collection.*

Born about 1869, William was the eldest son of Nathan DeWitt Bachman and Nancy Johnathan "Johnnie" Davis. At least three more sons followed: Edward Kelsey (born 1871), Nathan Dulaney (1873) and George Tipton (1875). At least four daughters were also born to the union: Mary Powell (1878), Pauline Davis (1880), Annie Laurie (1882) and Cornellia "Nell" Ellen (1885).

Born on December 26, 1844, Nathan DeWitt Bachman was a Confederate veteran of the Civil War, having enlisted on May 15, 1861, at the age of just sixteen. Serving for the duration of the war in several units of the Third Tennessee Regiment, by the war's end, Bachman had attained the rank of sergeant major. On April 9, 1865, Sergeant Major Bachman surrendered to Union troops at the war's closing battle in Appomattox Courthouse, Virginia. Following the war, he became the county clerk of Sullivan County, Tennessee. In 1868, he married "Johnnie" Davis.[1]

By 1907, eldest son William J. Bachman was employed by the Pacific Mutual Life Insurance Company within the firm of Howell and Bachman, of which he was co-owner. William was married, and the couple had two young daughters. The happy family lived on Windsor Avenue in Bristol.

**BACHMAN'S TRUNK
CONTAINED JEWELS**

Wife Gets Back Personal Effects
of One of the Columbia's
Victims.

BAD LUCK IN CALIFORNIA

He and Several of His Kinspeople
Come to Ill in Western
Travel.

WILLIAM J. BACHMAN.

William, along with his father and his brother Edward, were devoted Freemasons. Members of King Lodge No. 461 in Bristol, William had twice been elected to the chair of Eminent Commander of the St. Omer Commandery of Knights Templar.[2] Edward served as the Most Worshipful Grand Master of the Grand Lodge of Tennessee in 1909. William was reportedly in attendance at a grand meeting of Masonic lodges in Nashville, Tennessee, at the end of January 1907.[3]

Evidence of William's strong work ethic and dedication to Pacific Mutual Life is given by the fact that his journey to the Pacific coast—and his voyage aboard the *Columbia*—was an all-expense-paid reward from the company for having been one of the very few agents to have written sufficient insurance in 1906 to entitle him to the free trip; he was, in fact, the only agent east of the Mississippi River to have been so rewarded. Bachman was said to have been very proud of the compliment, not only because of the pleasure he anticipated but also because his vacation was won by way of a contest that tested his merits as an insurance solicitor.[4]

Noted as being a man who "practiced as he preached," William carried life insurance totaling $25,000—$5,000 in his own company, a $15,000 policy taken out with Preferred Accident shortly before his journey and a $5,000 policy with Farm Mutual.[5]

William J. Bachman departed Bristol for what would, tragically, be the final time on July 1, 1907.[6] His wife and two young daughters left for Colby, in Sullivan County, Tennessee, to stay with relatives until his return. It was noted that were the trip not a hard-earned reward, William would have likely never made such a journey.[7]

Bachman's movements and the itinerary of his trip are largely unknown, though a few details are available. On his arrival in San Francisco on July 18, 1907, William penned a humorous postcard to his business partner, Dr. J.F. Howell, in which he joked that he had "struck 'Frisco" fifteen months after the famous 1906 earthquake, "but of course not nearly so hard." He also

Above: In 1907, the Bachman family was living on Windsor Avenue in Bristol, Tennessee. *Author's collection.*

Left: A devoted Freemason, William J. Bachman was a member of King Lodge No. 461 in Bristol, Tennessee. *Author's collection.*

Opposite: Columbia became interred in a heavy ice field in January 1907. Captain Peter Doran is seated on the left in the foreground. *Author's collection.*

noted that he would be sailing for Portland, Oregon, aboard the *Columbia*. Dr. Howell did not receive the postcard until July 25.[8]

William Bachman boarded the *Columbia* in San Francisco on Saturday, July 20, 1907, as a first-class passenger. Seeing him off at the pier was Zeno T. Harris, a Memphis, Tennessee agent for the Pacific Mutual Life Insurance Company who had accompanied Bachman to San Francisco and as far west as Los Angeles. Harris may have briefly boarded the *Columbia* himself, as he knew the precise location of his associate's cabin: on the lower deck, port side.[9]

Prior to the vessel's departure, Bachman took the time to write a postcard to his family confirming his sailing plans. The postcard, along with several others penned at unknown points along his journey, was received on July 22.[10]

As a first-class passenger, William would have had a comfortable folding berth in a paneled cabin outfitted in a manner similar to that of Pullman railway cars. And of course lighting was provided by the ship's famous incandescent bulbs, though by 1907, the system had been upgraded from Edison's original installation. If Bachman wished for his berth's light to be turned off, he would have needed to summon a steward, who would then have to unlock a rosewood box outside the cabin in order to extinguish the light.

William would have dined in the first-class saloon, an elegant room paneled in maple, French walnut and Hungarian ash. A large shade of

Bohemian glass featured an electric light. Other electric lighting fixtures of frosted glass also adorned the saloon.

Bachman's exact movements and activities aboard the *Columbia*'s brief final voyage will remain forever unknown.

As dusk descended on the evening of July 20, the *Columbia*, under the command of Captain Peter Doran, became enshrouded in fog. The vessel was carrying approximately 251 passengers and crew. Due to reportedly heavy rolling, many of the passengers were afflicted with seasickness and, nauseated, had taken to their berths early that evening.

Despite the thick shroud of fog and moderately rough seas, the *Columbia*'s speed was not reduced. Adding to the disconcerting effect of the fog was the blaring whistle of a nearby schooner. This unseen vessel was the *San Pedro*. Loaded with a cargo of 390,000 feet of redwood lumber, the *Pedro* also neglected to reduce speed.

At 12:22 a.m. on July 21, 1907, the *San Pedro* dramatically charged from behind the curtain of fog on a direct course for the *Columbia*. On the bridge, Captain Doran ordered his engines fully reversed. But it was too late to avoid the oncoming schooner. A collision was inevitable. With great force, *San Pedro* penetrated *Columbia*'s starboard side. During the collision, Doran, in exasperation, shouted to the *Pedro*, "What are you doing, man?!"

The passenger steamer immediately began to sink. The smaller schooner, though its bow was heavily damaged, maintained buoyancy, in part due to its cargo of timber.

The location of Bachman's first-class cabin aboard the *Columbia* offered to some in 1907 a clue as to how he met his untimely death in the sinking. It was reported that this portion of the lower deck was where the *San Pedro* penetrated, with William's cabin being within the area of severe damage. It was believed at the time that he had been killed in the collision itself, rather than having drowned.[11] But this could not have been the case, as the *San Pedro* penetrated the *Columbia*'s starboard, rather than its port, side. With the collision occurring at 12:22 a.m., the entire sinking transpiring in mere minutes and accounts stating that many passengers were confined to their berths with seasickness, it remains probable that William was in his cabin asleep or sick at the time, leaving him with little or no chance of escape.

Immediately following the collision, Captain Doran ordered the *Columbia*'s lifeboats filled and lowered. Though several of the lifeboats were successfully launched, the crew simply did not have enough time. In less than ten minutes, the once-heralded *Columbia* vanished beneath the waves,

This postcard shows the *George W. Elder*, one of the first vessels to come to the aid of *Columbia*'s survivors. *Author's collection.*

taking with it eighty-eight passengers and crew, including nearly every child on board. In the final seconds of the sinking, it was reported that the ocean's surface was roiled by a mighty explosion, believed to have been caused by the bursting of one of the ship's boilers.

A number of survivors actually managed to swim to the swamped decks of the *San Pedro*. Soon, two other steamers, the *George W. Elder* and the *Roanoke*, were on the scene. In the end, approximately 163 survivors were rescued from the *Columbia*. The *George W. Elder* took the *San Pedro*, miraculously still afloat, under tow to the shore.

News of the sinking of the *Columbia* and the resultant loss of eighty-eight lives was extensively covered in the press nationwide. In Bristol, Bachman's relatives anxiously awaited confirmation that he had been aboard the ill-fated steamer. Confirmation arrived the following day, July 22, in the form of the postcards William wrote prior to boarding the vessel.[12] Zeno T. Harris was contacted by the Pacific Mutual Life Insurance Company, and he telegraphed verification that he had seen Bachman off at the pier.

William J. Bachman's family and friends, noting the absence of his name on survivor lists printed in the newspapers, immediately feared the worst. On the morning of July 23, William's brother Edward took on the heartrending task of telephoning his sister-in-law in Colby, Tennessee, informing her of the sinking of the *Columbia* and her husband's probable fate. Mrs. Bachman,

Roanoke, one of *Columbia*'s primary rescuers, appears to be making speed in this view from 1911. *Author's collection.*

weighed down with the news that she was now in all probability a widow, returned with her daughters to Bristol on the evening of July 25.[13]

By July 25, William's father, Nathan D. Bachman, had abandoned hope of ever seeing his son alive again and was instead focusing on the hope of bringing his body home for burial. The family contacted Samuel I. Boring, a resident of Los Angeles and a childhood friend of William's, requesting that he please proceed at once to Eureka, California, where the recovered bodies of the *Columbia*'s dead were to be brought ashore, in order that he might be able to identify his lost friend. Boring was in a good position to do so, as he had just met up with William Bachman when the latter briefly visited Los Angeles. The two old friends had reminisced about their shared childhoods.[14]

Accurate descriptions of William were wired to the Freemasons of San Francisco and the corporate headquarters of the Pacific Mutual Life Insurance Company, with both groups readily agreeing to provide any possible aid in the search. William Bachman was described as smooth-shaven, with "three or four" false upper teeth, worn in the front and attached to a plate extending over the roof of his mouth. His clothing was said to be marked, and if William had been wearing his coat and vest, it was reported, there would be identification papers in these articles of clothing. Bachman's family stated to the press that they would be willing to expend almost any amount of money were it to help in the recovery of their loved one.[15]

William's parents reportedly received another one of his last-minute postcards on July 26. It reaffirmed his sailing plans.[16]

By July 31, 1907, the Bachman family had relinquished their desire to bring William back home to Bristol. The previous day, Edward K. Bachman was the recipient of a telegram from the San Francisco and Portland Steamship Company, operators of the *Columbia*. It stated that, due to the limitations of diving at the time, they would be unable to recover the bodies of the ship's lost passengers and crew.[17] The lack of bodies found floating on the ocean's surface reinforces the theory that the majority of those lost in the sinking were belowdecks when the *Columbia* disappeared. Dr. C.S. Butler of Bristol, who had once taken soundings of the area of the Pacific Ocean where the ship was lost, noted that "it is the one place of uneven depths along the Pacific coast, the surface indicating that the water has submerged a mountain, with great ravines and deep coves." Dr. Butler felt it was quite likely that the *Columbia* went down in water a mile deep, as he had found places of that depth and other places which he was unable to fathom.[18]

As it turned out, California had held tragic fates for the Bachman family for many years. William's great-uncle Joseph Bachman sailed from San Francisco in 1850, bound for New York City. From that day forth, nothing more was heard from him, nor of the vessel on which he sailed. Another great-uncle, Nathan L. Bachman, a wealthy mine owner residing in Fresno, California, was murdered "by Chinese" soon after the end of the Civil War. His son, also named Nathan, left immediately for Fresno to settle his father's estate, but he soon took ill and unexpectedly passed away within a few weeks. A first cousin of William J. Bachman was in two bad railway accidents in California while serving in the Eleventh Infantry Regiment. The train carrying the soldiers was wrecked on the way to the coast, and the corresponding train, carrying the same soldiers on their return from the Philippines, was involved in a collision. More recently, two of William's sisters (unnamed in the press article) had narrowly escaped drowning. It was reported that one of the sisters had swum out beyond her depth, and the other sister, in an effort to rescue her, was "about to go down for the last time" when a Good Samaritan came to their rescue and saved them both.[19]

Though his body was never recovered, the story of William J. Bachman does have a touching epilogue. In early August 1907, a trunk belonging to Bachman, recovered from the vicinity of the *Columbia*'s sinking, arrived at the home of Zeno T. Harris in Memphis, Tennessee. Harris was the gentleman who had seen Bachman off at the pier, and the trunk was sent to him by mistake. Found within the trunk were numerous souvenirs that William had

This monument marks the Bachman family plot in Glenwood Cemetery, Bristol, Tennessee. William's body was never recovered. *Author's collection.*

purchased as gifts for his friends and family back home in Bristol, including a number of items for his fellow Freemasons. Each was thoughtfully labeled with the name of their intended recipient. Harris forwarded the trunk to Bristol, where Edward K. Bachman undertook the solemn task of distributing his brother's posthumous gifts.[20]

The Bachman family rests together in their large family plot in Glenwood Cemetery in Bristol, Tennessee. Of course, William J. Bachman is not with them physically, nor does the plot contain a cenotaph in his memory. It is as though he truly vanished with the SS *Columbia* on July 21, 1907.

2

RMS *LUSITANIA*

Next to the RMS *Titanic*, the Cunard Line's RMS *Lusitania* might very well be the most famous ocean liner in history. For many decades, elementary-school children in the United States have been taught erroneously that the sinking of the ship at the hands of a German submarine on May 7, 1915, is the reason their country entered the monstrous conflict of World War I. Regrettably, this myth is the primary reason that most laypeople today know the ship at all. In fact, though the horrific act, with the resultant loss of 128 American lives, did much to turn the hearts and minds of U.S. citizens further against Germany, it was not a deciding factor in our entering the war. But in its own time, the oceangoing greyhound *Lusitania* was a queen of the seas.

Lusitania was constructed by the shipbuilding firm John Brown & Company in Clydebank, Scotland, between 1904 and 1906. The construction of this mammoth new steamship—787 feet in length—and its sister ship, RMS *Mauretania*, was funded by a grant from the British government with the provision that both vessels could be requisitioned for use as auxiliary cruisers if needed during a time of war. Boasting unbounded comfort and luxury, and designed with an airy, open feel, the *Lusitania* was capable of making an impressive twenty-five knots per hour.

With its maiden voyage in 1907, the ship was an immediate success, quickly becoming a favorite of the elite transatlantic traveler, or anyone who needed to make the crossing quickly. For a certain banker from Tazewell,

An artist's rendering of the *Lusitania* speeding across the North Atlantic adorns this postcard from the early 1900s. *Author's collection.*

Virginia, in the fall of 1908, the *Lusitania* would provide transportation to renewed health during a dire time in his life.

SAMUEL HENRY PRESTON

Born on May 28, 1865, Samuel Henry Preston served as the cashier of the old Bank of Clinch Valley in Tazewell. The year 1906, and leading into 1907, was progressing well not only for the *Lusitania* but also for the bank. In January 1907, Preston reported that the bank's business was "about the same, perhaps a little better."[21]

As the *Lusitania* was establishing its stellar reputation on the North Atlantic run, Henry Preston was stricken by illness. In late July 1908, he was noted as having been "right ill for several days."[22] The next day's newspaper elaborated that Preston had been "confined to his home" by his illness.[23]

One week later, he was still suffering. By now, a diagnosis had been determined: typhoid fever. The local newspaper noted that "it is hoped by his many friends that no serious complications will arise or dangerous symptoms develop."[24] Caused by infection with the bacterium *Salmonella enterica typhi*, typhoid fever is a severe illness and was much more so in 1908, a time before antibiotics. The sufferer is plagued by high fevers, muscular weakness, extreme fatigue, weight loss due to loss of appetite and severe gastrointestinal upset, among other symptoms. In short, Samuel Henry Preston was miserable.

On September 17, nearly two months after Preston's illness began, the *Tazewell Republican* reported that he had recovered sufficiently to enable him to come to town "for brief visits."[25]

Henry Preston was very likely still feeling overwhelming fatigue following his battle with typhoid fever. On October 1, it was reported that he and his wife, Martha Josephine, had traveled to New York, where they would be spending several weeks before returning to Virginia to visit a Mr. and Mrs. A. Cummins.[26] It was not uncommon at this time for travel to be prescribed by a physician or undertaken of one's own volition in an effort to improve one's health. The trip that would follow for the Prestons presents a perfect example of someone at the time "taking the cure," as this form of travel was known.

By mid-October 1908, Mr. and Mrs. Preston had decided to go abroad for a while, undoubtedly with Henry's health in mind. While a passenger on a steamship off the coast of Ireland, Henry wrote a letter to the editor of the *Tazewell Republican*, which was published in part on October 22, 1908.

Have experienced a most enjoyable voyage, and feel that I've about regained my usual health. Have stood the trip well, enjoy a fine appetite, digestion good, and never felt better in my life. Evidently no mistake was made in deciding on a sea voyage. We are off the coast of Ireland now, expect to touch Queenstown tonight, and arrive at Liverpool tomorrow (Friday). We are booked through to Paris, and upon our return shall "do" England, Scotland and Ireland.[27]

Following their European sojourn, Henry and Josephine booked a second-class passage home onboard the *Lusitania*, boarding at Queenstown, Ireland, on October 25, 1908.[28] As second-class passengers, the Prestons would have been sailing in comfortable—even luxurious—surroundings that would have rivaled, or even surpassed, first-class travel on older steamships. Located within an isolated deckhouse in the stern of the ship, second-class accommodations included a spacious dining saloon with overhead balcony, a communal lounge, a smoking room intended as a haven for the men and an elegant drawing room with the ladies in mind.

Mr. and Mrs. Preston arrived at Pier 54 in New York City on October 30. From there, they made their way back to their home on Tower Street in

Lusitania is here seen on November 20, 1908, warping into Pier 54 in New York, one month after the Prestons arrived aboard it. *Library of Congress, Prints and Photographs Division.*

Tazewell. Henry told the local press that he "never felt better physically in his life."[29]

The continued popularity of both the *Lusitania* and *Mauretania* is demonstrated by the fact that in 1910 a church in Roanoke, Virginia, passed a church attendance contest centering on the two ocean greyhounds.

> *A very interesting race was partly finished last Sunday in the No. 7 Hustlers class of Calvary Baptist Sunday school.*
>
> *The class was divided into two factions and one side was called the* Mauretania *crew, with H.M. Figgatt, captain, while the other side took the name of* Lusitania *crew, with R.V. Fowlkes as captain. The two ships started from Norfolk on a 5900-mile "Trip to Palestine" in January and last Sunday the* Mauretania *crew landed in Palestine, with the* Lusitania *bunch hot on their trail.*
>
> *The conditions of the race were that each new scholar should count 100 miles and each one present 10 miles. For every member absent 10 miles was deducted. The two crews decided last Sunday that they would race back on attendance, that is, let each one present count 50 miles and deduct same for each one absent. In this way they hope to retain those new members brought in on the first half of the race.*

The class started out with 28 members and it has increased its roll now to 144. The race was watched with much enthusiasm in the Sunday school.[30]

On May 7, 1915, nearly seven years after the Prestons took their memorable journey, the *Lusitania* was torpedoed and sunk by the German U-boat *U-20* in the Irish Sea. The tragedy took only eighteen minutes to unfold and resulted in the deaths of 1,198 men, women and children. In Tazewell, Samuel Henry Preston was asked by a local journalist to reminisce about his 1908 voyage on the ill-fated ship, a conversation that revealed more details of his and Josephine's voyage home.

The loss of the ship Lusitania, *which was torpedoed by a German submarine last Friday, is keenly felt by Mr. and Mrs. Henry Preston, of this town, who, on their return from abroad a few years ago, traveled on the ship, and remember so well its magnificent appointments, and the courtesy and consideration of its officers. Mr. Preston carries a souvenir of this trip on the boat in the shape of a broken piece of china, which he picked up on deck just after a severe storm, when china and other breakable things were smashed by the pitching of the boat. He recalls vividly this incident, brought to his mind so forcibly by the fact that his physical condition was such at that time that he didn't care if she did go down.*[31]

CHARLES FROHMAN

Among the more prominent of the *Lusitania*'s victims was the famous theater producer Charles Frohman. Theatergoers in the region of Southwest Virginia would have recognized his name in connection with several of the plays he produced and that had been performed in regional cities. On Wednesday, March 22, 1911, the Academy in Roanoke featured Miss Billie Burke—who in 1939 would be immortalized as Glenda the Good Witch of the North in *The Wizard of Oz*—starring in Frohman's hit comedy *Suzanne*.[32] The Academy would also showcase Frohman's *The Conspiracy* in October 1913.[33]

Rita Jolivet, seen here in a 1904 publicity print, recreated her dramatic ordeal on the *Lusitania* for the 1918 film *Lest We Forget. Author's collection.*

SS *SIBERIA*

Grady Garrett, a former Salem and Roanoke newspaper journalist, was at sea aboard the SS *Siberia* when news of the *Lusitania*'s torpedoing broke. He briefly recalled the incident in his travel diary: "A daily sheet giving all the more important wireless news of the world was published on the steamer. The news of the sinking of the *Lusitania*, May 7, caused much excitement among the passengers, while the death of John Bunny several days before occasioned genuine regret."[34]

THE DANGER ZONE

While the United States did not join World War I until April 6, 1917, nearly two years after the *Lusitania* was sunk, Southwest Virginians were finding out long before just how heated things had become overseas. A group from Roanoke, Virginia, traveling abroad in August 1914, just after the outbreak of war, returned home aboard the RMS *Baltic* with a remarkable and detailed firsthand account for the local newspaper. The following report was printed in the *World-News* on August 24, 1914:

> *A reporter for* The Roanoke Times *had an engagement with Mr. Edward L. Stone at 9 o'clock last evening and expected a long, succinct narrative, but at that hour callers were yet coming to the Stone home on Ninth Avenue and Mr. Stone was unable to give the reporter more than three-quarters of an hour, during which he gave an interesting review of the main circumstances of the party's flight from the trouble zone.*
>
> *Everyone was in good spirits when their train arrived Sunday, but all were travel strained and weary and the only lull in the home-coming receptions were when those who held the center of interest were compelled to seek refreshing naps during the afternoon.*
>
> *Two points in Mr. Stone's narrative and his views on the situation are especially worthy of mention. While the party has traveled only in America and in countries at present at war with Germany, and did not study causes or have any special interest in the ways and wherefores of the European turmoil, the members could not fail to notice that everywhere the sentiment seemed practically unanimous that it is a case of Germany gone mad.*
>
> *Naturally, it is pointed out, the Roanokers had little opportunity to hear a German expression on the situation and the result of observation*

as to sentiment is based purely on what they saw and heard under these conditions.

The second point is that the hue and cry raised against the steerage accommodations furnished returning Americans, by the White Star Line at least, is not so well founded. Mr. Stone is emphatic in his statement that the returning refugees bought steerage passages and that the steerage accommodations they received were fully up to anything they could expect, plus continuous and earnest efforts of the Baltic's company to ameliorate the disadvantages and discomforts in every way possible.

Mr. and Mrs. Cassell were able to secure second cabin accommodations from the first, but Mr. and Mrs. Stone, Miss Stone and Miss Fishburn left Liverpool traveling steerage. The ladies were fortunate in securing first cabin accommodations after the first night out and Mr. Stone received promotion after two nights below.

Mr. Stone says he was not at all disappointed or disgruntled at the accommodations afforded. Certainly, he says, the conditions under which meals were served were somewhat revolting to persons accustomed to more genteel surroundings, but these conditions were due almost wholly to the fact that the usual steerage passengers had to be accommodated at the time and place and not through any lack of endeavor on the part of the ship's company to make things as comfortable as possible for those who were out of their element below decks.

Officers granted passengers who were strangers to the steerage all the liberty of promenading upper decks that they could without a rank violation of the ship's discipline and the immigration regulations. Those above who had friends or acquaintances below aided the officers by inviting the steerage passengers to their cabins for lunches, sending baskets of food below and otherwise making their unfortunate shipmates as comfortable as possible under the circumstances.

Some Americans on the Baltic, Mr. Stone says, really made themselves obnoxious sending up loud complaints against their steerage surroundings and seemed not to realize that first cabin comforts are not to be had in the steerage, no matter what the conditions.

The Stone-Cassell party, composed of Mr. and Mrs. James C. Cassell and son, J.C. Cassell, Jr.; Mr. and Mrs. Edward L. Stone and daughter, Miss Mary; Miss Evelyn Fishburn and Mr. Robert Allen. They sailed from New York July 1, on the Aquitania, landing at Fishguard after an uneventful voyage. Fishguard is the channel port where London passengers are lightered from vessels bound for Liverpool.

After a week in London, whence the party proceeded after landing, three weeks were spent motoring through Southern England and Wales. Returning to London for two days, the party started for Paris, motoring from London to Folkstone and from Boulogne to the French capital. Two days after their arrival in Paris the situation began to look threatening. Mr. Cassell came into the hotel from a trip about the city and suggested that as conditions were so uncertain it was best to return to London. The ladies were more or less anxious to escape any inconvenience, so the start back to London was made Saturday, August 1.

The only real trouble the party encountered was on this trip. The railway station at Paris was congested beyond description and all was confusion in the transportation world. "It took us an hour to gain a hundred feet in our effort to get a train for Boulogne," said Mr. Stone. Finally, seeing that attention to baggage would hamper proceedings, he instructed his courier, one whom he engaged on a previous visit abroad, ten years ago, to follow on the next train with the luggage and the party then proceeded forward to their train without the necessity of worrying with baggage.

London was reached without mishap at 1 o'clock Sunday morning and the baggage and conductor came in a few hours later. Then followed a two weeks wait for a chance to leave England.

Mr. Stone says the party first had passage engaged on the Vaterland. This sailing was cancelled. Then they booked for the Alsatian. This sailing did not occur. The Carmania offered another chance, but it failed of maturity. The fourth try with the Baltic was successful, and catch-as-catch-can reservations secured by merest chance, finally brought the travelers to New York.

Nowhere were the experiences of the party, so far as personal comfort is concerned, of such a nature as to be termed eventful. At no time was it necessary to make any special demands on the American diplomatic representatives abroad, although several conferences were had with ministers in both Paris and London on unimportant points.

"When we reached Paris," Mr. Stone said, "the Caillaux trial was nearing an end and occupied the public attention almost to the exclusion of any other subject, and the day that the slayer of Calmette was acquitted, the street scenes were remarkable. But in a short time came the war clouds and the tragedy and its ending was forgotten in an instant. Overnight the Paris of bright lights and gaiety that we read of disappeared, and in its place arose a military Paris, all earnestness and anxious to be in the fight."

There was no excitement; no hysteria; no aimless running here and there, but all clock-like movements of military organizations. Cavalry clattered through the streets which a day before had been given over to promenaders and motorists. Infantry moved like companies of automatons, so perfect was the drill and discipline. At the transportation terminals there was congestion of course, but it was not aimless. Every person either was going to war or getting away from war, and apparently no man who had a blood interest in France was among the latter class.

"There was never any fear of personal violence in our party," said Mr. Stone. "The night before we left Paris, we went to several shows and at midnight to a fashionable restaurant. The latter place was deserted. Waiters had torn off their aprons and gone to join the colors, while we found later that another reason for the deserted condition was that a man had been killed in the place earlier in the evening."

An interesting financial deal was a part of the party's experience in London. Coming out of France, all hands combined brought about 4,000 francs paper. They could not spend it in France, unless they bought enough to "kill a bill," as shopkeepers and others positively refused to give up coin in change.

The courier who brought the baggage over had a Turkish tobacconist friend in London and knowing that his clients were overloaded with French paper, he negotiated a par exchange for a part of the paper; the Turk giving gold for the notes. When the Americans learned of this the next day, they sent the remainder of the franc notes to the same source of exchange, but money matters had reached the stage where the best that could be done by the friendly Ottoman was to discount the bills at 75 percent, giving gold in exchange. This deal, however, relieved all fear of trouble about ready money, and as soon as the English government issued several million pounds of one-pound "shin-platers," some of which Mr. Stone brought home with him, good for any current needs, there was no more money troubles.

Even American gold certificates were not worth the ink they were printed with, so far as getting coin in exchange for them in Paris was concerned. Sellers of accommodations or commodities would take the entire bill, but there was nothing doing on purchases that required specie change.

Mr. Stone was present at the organization of the American Relief Committee in London. Very few of the American travelers who carried substantial letters of credit of travelers checks had any difficulty supplying their needs eventually, but thousands of tourists who were traveling on an economical basis and had little money to spend outside of a fixed schedule, found themselves absolutely penniless when unexpected conditions entailed added expense, and it was this class more than any other that the committee sought to aid, although many wealthy persons were given temporary accommodation.

In London the time was spent watching the preparations for war, which were equally as interesting as those noted in Paris. The London papers, by agreement with the war office, did not publish any details of troop movements and the Londoners were kept completely in the dark. They saw their soldiers mobilizing and moving to the English Channel, but never a word as what was being done beyond, or what the scope of the military operations would be.

When the state department, in an effort to learn the circumstances of the Stone party on request of Roanoke friends, cabled the embassy at London, the American consular agents did not know where to find the travelers, and an agency with which Mr. Stone and others had some business notified him of an advertisement placed by the consul in London papers, seeking information.

In London, Mr. Stone says, military enthusiasm is intense. Men literally overrun the recruiting stations and there does not seem to be any sacrifice that the Britons are not eager to make, to further the objects of the operations of the war office.

Before sailing, the Roanokers learned that the magnificent Aquitania, *on which they sailed from New York, had been converted into a transport by the government. Four thousand men, it was said, were placed aboard the ship and swept it clean of the magnificent fixtures, tore out all unnecessary woodwork and within a few days transformed a passenger liner of the first-class into a dingy transport for men and horses.*

The Roanokers heard before they left London of how the French government provided a special train for the safe transport of the German ambassador from Paris, to the frontier. When arrived at the boundary the Germans not only took charge of their returning ambassador, but also the French train.

Mr. Stone says he was particularly impressed with the absolute earnestness with which the French went about the mobilization work. There seemed on the face of every soldier one saw an unusual look of determination, such as is seen on the face of any man who has a serious duty ahead, knows how to perform it in the quickest and most businesslike manner.

The home-coming yesterday ended a journey that started in London, the 12th. The party left London for Liverpool that day and sailed on the Baltic, *the 13th. It was understood by those aboard the* Baltic *before the vessel landed that it had been convoyed by British cruisers all the way, although the warships were never in sight until one passed the* Baltic, *going back to sea, when near New York.*

Mr. Allen was fortunate in securing earlier passage than the Baltic. *He left Plymouth on the* New Amsterdam, *on the 10th, and reached New York early last week. From there he went to visit his mother at Chautauqua Lake, and joined the Stone party in New York yesterday for the return journey to Roanoke.*

At the Stone home, Miss Catherine Stone had decorated a reception room on the lower floor with American flags, with a "welcome" arch near the hall entrance, and it was this bank of Star Spangled Banners that greeted the returning tourists when they reached the residence.[35]

One month later, another Roanoke resident, John B. Retallack, faced a much more harrowing ordeal. He was taken for a spy in Cologne, Germany! His extraordinary story was published in the *World-News* on September 30, 1914.

Casting his lot in Cologne, Germany as a workman in a massive electrical plant, where he hoped to learn German ideas and become efficient as an electrical engineer, John B. Retallack, formerly of St. Louis, now of Roanoke, was compelled to leave the continent, a refugee, after experiencing many hardships and peculiar and interesting adventures.

He was twice arrested and once imprisoned as a spy by German soldiers.

To a reporter for The Roanoke Times, *Mr. Retallack last night told of his experiences: how he was arrested on one occasion as a spy, kept in a German military prison, and of many humorous and pathetic results of the great conflagration which now involves eight great world nations. He left New York in May this year, sailing on the White Star steamer* Olympic, *and ten days later docked at Southampton, England. It was his purpose, he said, to seek his fortune in Germany, where he hoped to learn the electrical business. After brief sojourns in London and Paris the young soldier of fortune journeyed to Cologne, where he soon secured a position with Siemen's Electrical Company. He was aided in his venture by a native friend. Under his new employers the young American worked faithfully, adapting himself to his new surroundings, making new friends and what is more learning the great German language. Time passed quickly, and soon upon the horizon appeared the great war cloud, ominous and threatening. But the German people, it appeared, were rather expecting it.*

RMS *Olympic* and its ill-fated sister, *Titanic*, were the White Star Line's response to Cunard's ocean greyhounds. *Author's collection.*

August 2 the event which will go down into history as an epoch of world-wide importance occurred on the Continental stage, when Germany and England found themselves "at war" with each other.

"I was living in a boarding house," said Mr. Retallack, speaking of the breaking out of the war. "When the news became known, bulletins were posted all over Cologne that foreigners must leave the city at once. I left my boarding house and went to the home of a German friend, where I stayed two days. He told me I might remain with him until it was learned what the import of the order concerning the foreigners might be. When my two days were up I returned to my boarding house. When I went to the door I was met by my former landlord, a big German.

"'Stop,' he said, 'and wait here a minute.'

"I waited outside the door. He went in. After he had been in the house a few moments, it occurred to me there was something suspicious about his actions. I tried the door, and found it locked. A few minutes later I found myself in the hands of the police. They caught me by the wrist and escorted me to the jail. There I was searched, and when my passport, which I had obtained as soon as the war became imminent, was found, I had no difficulty, and was released.

"The next day I determined to leave the continent, so I went to Brussels, thinking that I would be safe there, as I understood it was considered neutral territory by all the nations. I stopped in a Brussels hotel several days. By that time I learned of the fighting around Liege. From Brussels I turned into Holland, having in mind to try to reach England. However, in Holland, I learned that the foreigners were not being disturbed in Cologne and that it was safe to return there. I left and went back to the German city, thinking I might be able to return to work.

"But there was no work to be found. All German able bodied men were being called to arms. Industries of every description ceased operation. The women took the places of the men. On street cars in Cologne I saw women handling the street cars, women cleaning the streets, and young maidens, thirteen and fourteen years old, carrying mail.

"The mobilization of soldiers was the greatest site [sic] I ever saw. It was conducted without a flaw, and worked out like clockwork. Men who thought they were going to work early in the morning found themselves uniformed and equipped, on the march to the front by nightfall."

"When were you arrested as a spy?" Mr. Retallack was asked.

"When I returned to Cologne. Of course I went to another boarding house, rather than face the suspicions of my former landlord, who betrayed me to the police. One afternoon I was watching the soldiers march along the streets, and was especially interested in the artillery. The houses, as you know, in Cologne, as in many German cities, are built flush to the streets, and as I watched the magnificent artillery equipment it occurred to me to snap a picture of the scene with a camera which I had purchased in England on my way to the continent. I waited for a good chance and aiming my trusted instrument, snapped what I thought would prove 'a good one.'

"I had hardly done so before I found myself under military arrest. I had been seen by a soldier from the street. Troops marched me to the military prison, where I was placed in a cell. I wondered what my fate would be. In the meantime, my camera and its film were confiscated. The film was developed and the film showed not only a picture I had taken of the artillery, but a beautiful one of a Zeppelin airship cruising above Cologne, which I had snapped a few days before. That looked pretty bad for me; but with my valuable passport and with the aid of the American consul I was released, after being incarcerated for twenty-four hours."

"How was the fare in prison?" he was asked.

"It was not so bad; and I was not badly treated by the soldiers. I don't think any harm would have been done me unless it had become generally *known that I had taken the pictures, then, perhaps, a mob might have gotten after my skin."*

"When I got on my train at Cologne," he said, "the train was full. I hardly knew where I would get a seat. The continental trains are not like ours. They have compartments. As I walked up the platform looking for a likely one, I was hailed by a German who could speak a little English. When I entered his compartment, I learned he was a wounded soldier returning from the battle of Liege. He had been wounded in the neck with a lance. He told me he knew I was an American as soon as he saw me, and as he knew a little English wanted to practice it on me. We had an interesting conversation, and he recited, what he termed, 'Belgian and French atrocities.'

"The soldier recounted occasions in Belgian cities of German soldiers going to the door of a Belgian citizen to ask for food and being shot down in their tracks by women and maidens, who used guns from windows and housetops."

"A daring undertaking was performed by a body of Frenchmen, just outside Cologne," he said. "A number of them, disguised as German officers, secured themselves in four or five automobiles and attempted to seize an airship station near the outskirts of Cologne. Some of them were captured, however, and others made their escape. The result of the adventure was fruitless. I think the prisoners were executed.

"Of course," he continued, "rumors of all kinds circulated in Germany concerning the war, and Cologne was visited with as much of it as any other city. I heard many tales about the cruelty and atrocities of the allies. But, I believe, if the truth be known, that acts of indiscretion, cruelty, etc., brought on by the impulse of the time were committed by both sides. I am sure there are two sides to the question, and from my own experience, believe that the British side is given to American reading people more freely than the Kaiser's.

"I heard it told in Cologne that German airmen were fired on by French civilians sitting in front of Parisian cafes, but cannot vouch for the truthfulness of the report. Rumors like that and innumerable others were brought in by wounded soldiers returning from the front."

From Folkstone, Mr. Retallack journeyed to London, where he boarded the steamer Ruthenia, *of the Canadian Pacific lines. Great crowds of people were at the docks. Americans anxious to return home were waiting for a chance. American residents of London issued daily what was known as "The American Bulletin," on which was printed a list of steamers*

Lest We Forget, starring actress and *Lusitania* survivor Rita Jolivet, played at the Amuzu Theatre in Big Stone Gap on July 4, 1918. *Author's collection.*

and their time of leaving, quoting whether or not berths on them were available. Pickpockets had been doing their work earlier in the war, and about the wharves and docks were signs with the inscriptions: "Beware of pickpockets."

The Ruthenia *sailed to Montreal. The voyage over, according to Mr. Retallack, was uneventful. When the big vessel was nearing the Canadian coast, sailors in "the crow's nest" one night thought they detected "a light through the fog." Officers of the ship were called, but nothing could be learned of the light.*

"The passengers figured it out that the light was caused by an overdose of grog," said Mr. Retallack, smiling.

The vessel landed September 25, and the young American hurried South, where he found many friends waiting to welcome his return.

"What spoils of war did you leave behind?" he was asked, when the narrative turned to a humorous vein.

"So far as I remember," he replied, "I am minus a camera and a cello, which I had taken over with me. The authorities made me leave the musical instrument behind; I don't know why."

Summarizing his experiences the young soldier of fortune remarked that his adventure in Cologne is not regretted. His memories of the place are filled with many pleasures and many sorrows, but, after all of it, he is ready to cast his lot in the mountains of Virginia, where the skies are always clear and blue, where the flowers are prettiest, and where life is certainly more comfortable and more worth living.[36]

LEST WE FORGET

In the summer of 1918, just months before the November 11 ending of World War I, the film *Lest We Forget* was released. Loosely based on the sinking of the *Lusitania*, the film even starred one of its survivors, the popular actress Rita Jolivet. Residents of Southwest Virginia had several chances to watch the film. *Lest We Forget* played at the Amuzu Theatre in Big Stone Gap on July 4, 1918,[37] and the New Theatre in Tazewell booked the film one month later, on August 10.[38]

3

RMS *TITANIC*

Probably the most famous vessel in history besides Noah's ark, the RMS *Titanic*, lost on its maiden voyage on April 15, 1912, really requires no introduction. What most do not know is that among the 1,496 victims and 712 survivors, there were links to the region of Southwest Virginia.

ISIDOR STRAUS

Isidor Straus, co-owner of Macy's department store and a former member of the U.S. House of Representatives, was one of the *Titanic*'s most noted passengers. Isidor, alongside his beloved wife, Ida, achieved a romantic immortality with their deaths on the *Titanic*. During the evacuation, Ida refused to be separated from Isidor, famously proclaiming, "We have lived together for many years. Where you go, I go." Fans of the 1997 James Cameron film will undoubtedly remember the elderly couple lying on a bed in a tearful embrace as the ship sank. These were the Strauses, although this depiction is inaccurate, as the couple was reportedly last seen sitting beside each other in steamer chairs on the Boat Deck.

Future *Titanic* victim Isidor Straus gave a speech at Washington and Lee University in 1902. *Wikimedia Commons.*

Isidor Straus had a number of friends in Southwest Virginia.[39] A decade before his death at sea, Isidor gave a speech at Washington and Lee University in Lexington, Virginia, on Commencement Day, June 18, 1902. On that day, a portrait of the university's late president, William L. Wilson, was unveiled. Wilson and Straus had been close friends.[40]

During his speech, Isidor read the following letter sent to Wilson by President Grover Cleveland:

EXECUTIVE MANSION, WASHINGTON, AUGUST 13, 1894

My Dear Mr. Wilson,—I suppose a man very much depressed and disappointed may write a word of sympathy to another in like situation. We both hoped and wrought for better things; but now that we know our fate, I shall not let a moment pass before I acknowledge the great and unselfish work you have done in an attempt to bring about an honest and useful result.

Much has been developed which has shocked and surprised you and me; and I have within the last hour found myself questioning whether or not our party is a tariff reform party. This, however, is only temporary, and such feeling is quickly followed by my old trust in Democratic doctrines and the party which professes them.

But I only intend to express my sympathy with you and my gratitude for the fight you have made for real, genuine, tariff reform.

I hope now that you will be mindful of yourself and that you will try and repair a strained mental and physical condition by immediate care and rest.

Yours very sincerely,
[Signed] *"GROVER CLEVELAND."*
Hon. William L. Wilson.[41]

ELOISE HUGHES SMITH

On May 16, 1909, it was announced that Janie Slemp of Big Stone Gap, Virginia, a sister of Congressman Campbell Bascom Slemp, was to leave Philadelphia en route to Liverpool, England, on that date, for a summer abroad in Europe. Janie would not be alone on her journey. Accompanying her was to be fifteen-year-old Mary Eloise Hughes, daughter of Congressman James Anthony Hughes of Huntington, West Virginia. The pair of friends planned to visit England, Scotland, Ireland and France.[42]

Ellis Island records indicate that, after spending several months abroad, Eloise (as she preferred to be known) returned to the United States before Janie, arriving in New York onboard the SS *Roma* on October 6, 1909, having departed from Naples, Italy. Janie arrived in New York one month later, on November 1, aboard the RMS *Cretic*.

Titanic survivor Eloise Hughes Smith, here seen later in life, accompanied Susan Jane Slemp on a transatlantic journey in 1909. *Courtesy of Betsy Smith McLain.*

Nearly three years later, on February 8, 1912, Mary Eloise Hughes was wed to Lucian Philip Smith, a twenty-four-year-old gentleman from Morgantown, West Virginia, in Central Christian Church in Huntington. Among the ushers in this wedding stood another local connection: Dr. Henry Beckner, of Bluefield, Virginia.[43]

The newlywed Smiths had a marvelous honeymoon abroad, visiting Europe and Egypt. They departed New York as first-class passengers onboard the RMS *Olympic*, then the largest ship in the world, in February 1912. Come early April, they were ready to return home to West Virginia, and thus booked a first-class passage on *Olympic*'s brand-new sister, *Titanic*. In the ensuing tragedy, Lucian Philip Smith was one of the 1,496 victims. Eloise, now nearly two months pregnant, returned home a widow at the age of eighteen. Her story will continue elsewhere in this chapter.

ROBERT WILLIAMS DANIEL

Though his name is not recalled in Southwest Virginia today, *Titanic* survivor Robert Williams Daniel perhaps has the closest personal link to our region. He was a friend of Governor George C. Peery of Cedar Bluff. In fact, when Daniel entered politics himself in 1928, it was Governor Peery, along with Harry F. Byrd of Berryville, who appointed him to his first political position on the Advisory and Research Commission. Robert and Peery seem to have been good friends. In January 1934, Governor and Mrs. Peery and the

Daniels were even photographed together several times by the *Times-Dispatch* at a social event in Richmond. The fascinating life of this *Titanic* survivor who had friends in our area is worth recounting.

In a number of ways, Robert's life mirrored that of his father. Born on January 1, 1850, James Robertson Vivian Daniel was a highly praised attorney native to the city of Richmond, Virginia. It could be said that his successful legal career owed as much to genetics as to intelligence. James R.V. Daniel's father, Peter Vivian Daniel Jr., was also a widely known Richmond attorney and had at one time presided over the Richmond, Fredericksburg and Potomac Railroad. His father, the elder Peter Vivian Daniel, was also a man of high rank at the bar, having served as an associate justice of the United States Supreme Court from 1842 to 1860. And James's maternal great-grandfather was a figure of historic legal importance. Edmund Randolph was the first attorney general of the United States, a governor of Virginia and one of the most eminent lawyers in the nation's history.

Described by one contemporary as a "scholarly lawyer and modest, chivalrous man," James R.V. Daniel began his professional life as a civil engineer. He later abandoned that calling in order to follow in the footsteps of his ancestors. He attended the University of Virginia in Charlottesville and graduated from law school at Richmond College in 1873. James then traveled abroad for some time. On his return to the United States, he began to practice law with his father. Following the death of his father, James became associated with Edmund C. Minor and continued in that legal partnership until Minor's elevation to the bench. From that time forward, Daniel practiced law in Richmond, having an office in the Shaffer Building.

In 1883, James was united in marriage to Hallie Wise Williams. Born on August 15, 1859, the bride would go on to become a revered member of Richmond society and among the earliest members of the Richmond Women's Club.

On September 11, 1884, Hallie gave birth to the couple's first child. Likely in honor of his maternal grandfather, Robert F. Williams, the baby boy was named Robert Williams Daniel.

As a young man, Robert followed in his father's footsteps to the University of Virginia, from which he graduated in 1903. By the following year, he was employed in the traffic manager's office of the Richmond, Fredericksburg and Potomac Railroad, the company his grandfather had once presided over.

On November 25, 1904, while visiting friends in Yonkers, New York, James R.V. Daniel was stricken by an apoplectic stroke. On hearing the news of his illness, Hallie, along with twenty-year-old Robert, left Richmond for

James's bedside. Hardly had his family reached his side than, at 4:00 a.m. on November 26, James R.V. Daniel passed away. He was fifty-four years old.

Hallie had her husband's body brought home to 1001 Floyd Avenue in Richmond to lie in state until the funeral, which took place at 3:30 p.m. on Monday, November 29, at St. James Protestant Episcopal Church. James was laid to rest in the family plot in Hollywood Cemetery.

By this time, Robert had two siblings with whom to share the loss of their father: Channing Williams Daniel, born on March 18, 1890; and James Randolph Vivian Daniel, born on July 17, 1900. A sister, Mary Isabel Randolph Daniel, had been born on June 27, 1893, but, sadly, she died on July 17, 1900, at the age of seven. Her death was made even more tragic by the fact that her younger brother James was born the day Mary died.

Sometime in the following year, Robert entered the insurance business. He first became attached to the firm of Williams and Hart, eventually succeeding Mr. Williams as the district superintendent of the Maryland Life Insurance Company. In 1906, Robert and a fellow Maryland Life district superintendent, Charles Palmer Stearns, formed the firm Daniel and Stearns.

By 1911, Robert had embarked on his own business venture, the banking firm Robert W. Daniel and Company. Headquartered in Philadelphia, where Robert lived most of the time, there were also branches in New York and London.

The London branch of his firm made it necessary for Robert to occasionally traverse the North Atlantic to oversee business concerns. It was just such a journey aboard *Mauretania* that brought Robert to London's palatial Carlton Hotel. On the night of August 9, 1911, a fire erupted in the hotel, causing extensive damage and killing American actor Jameson Finney. Robert survived by clinging to a rope on a ledge and was credited with saving the life of an English friend.

The reason behind what would become Robert's most memorable voyage—his sixth crossing of the Atlantic—seems to have never been explicitly stated, but it can be assumed with reasonable certainty that business matters at the London branch of his banking firm was at least one factor.

Mixing business with pleasure, at some point during this journey Robert acquired a "prized" French bulldog. Naming the dog Gamin de Pycombe, he boarded the *Titanic* with his new bat-eared companion in Southampton on April 10, 1912. Robert's first-class cabin was on A Deck.

Robert Daniel survived the disaster that befell the new steamship, though debate continues over precisely how the young banker escaped. Some defend accounts he allegedly gave to newspapers in 1912. These accounts are generally quite extraordinary; in several, it was claimed that Robert swam through the freezing water completely nude until being pulled aboard a passing lifeboat.

It was later claimed that on this lifeboat Robert first met the newly widowed Eloise Hughes Smith. This terribly romantic detail seems to have gone without mention until at least August 1914 and is apocryphal. Neither Eloise nor anyone else in Lifeboat No. 6 is known to have mentioned picking up a survivor.

Though at this point we will likely never know precisely how Robert survived the sinking, recent research by myself, along with Randy Bryan Bigham and Rich Edwards, has led a number of people to conclude that he did, indeed, stay onboard the ship until the end, going into the frigid sea. He then swam to a lifeboat, potentially No. 4 or Collapsible A.

While aboard *Carpathia*, Robert sent a brief wireless message to his mother. "Safe. Expect to be in Richmond on Sunday." Hallie Daniel received the message on April 17, whereupon she and Channing left New York to meet the *Carpathia*. A cousin, widely known capitalist and railroad man John Skelton Williams, accompanied them.

RMS *Titanic* is seen here in its brief pre-disaster glory days. *Wikimedia Commons.*

There was an unsubstantiated report that Robert, who was noted as having an interest in wireless telegraphy, was some assistance to Harold Bride and Harold Cottam in sending the mountain of wireless messages.

Wearing a loose blue shirt and ridiculously large pants that would have been comical under any other circumstance, Robert Williams Daniel descended *Carpathia*'s gangplank. Draped across his arms was a pale young woman in a state of nervous hysteria. Robert thusly handed Eloise Hughes Smith over to her father, West Virginia congressman James Anthony Hughes, before making his way to his own entourage. The teenaged widow had made an impression on Robert, and he wouldn't forget her.

"After the *Titanic* disaster, he felt like he should have been dead, so he saw his remaining time as a second chance at life," Robert's daughter-in-law Linda Daniel said of his years after the *Titanic* disaster.

Whereas before he had been frugal with his considerable money, Robert began enjoying it, purchasing luxury items like racehorses and a yacht, the latter he used to cruise the Potomac River. He also took up card playing with a passion and avidly played the stock market.

Time passed, and the *Titanic* disaster faded from the headlines. Early in the spring of 1914, Robert was returning from his country home in Richmond to his primary residence in Philadelphia. He was asked by a friend to spend an evening in Washington, D.C., as a guest at an informal dinner party. He accepted.

Robert was to escort a Mrs. Smith, the hostess informed him. The hostess took him by the arm and walked with him to the other side of the room so that she might make her two guests acquainted. There undoubtedly followed a pleasant moment of surprise recognition. "But I already know Mr. Daniel," Eloise Hughes Smith smilingly informed the hostess. "We are old friends."

It was the beginning of a romance that would culminate in the only wedding between two *Titanic* survivors who did not know each other prior to the tragic voyage. The intimate ceremony, held in New York's Church of the Transfiguration on August 18, 1914, was a hushed affair.

Soon afterward, Robert had to depart his new bride for London to attend to business. While he was there, World War I erupted, leaving him marooned in England for some time.

By this time, Robert had replaced Gamin de Pycombe with another bulldog, this one being English. It was noted in March 1915 that the dog took the blue ribbon in a show in Philadelphia.

When the United States entered the war in April 1917, Robert and Eloise both took active roles to serve their country. By December 1917, Robert had helped to raise and organize a battalion for a home guard defense at Bryn Mawr and Rosemont, Pennsylvania. The group held several sham battles with other battalions, with Major Daniel's men winning many victories. Meanwhile, his *Titanic* bride studied nursing at the University Hospital in Richmond.

In February 1919, following the armistice, Captain Daniel was sent to France by the U.S. War Department as custodian of money to be used in exchanging the French currency of returning soldiers. He returned to the United States in March aboard the *Mauretania*.

On May 3, 1919, Captain Daniel, along with Brigadier General Herbert Lord, was presented with U.S. Treasury Department medals for their distinguished services.

By approximately 1920, the Daniels' marriage had crumbled. Following a separation of several years, Eloise was granted a divorce from Robert on March 20, 1923, in a domestic-relations court in Charleston, West Virginia. In her claim against Robert, Eloise cited an "unknown blonde woman." Robert did not protest the case. The decree obligated Eloise to not remarry for six months and Robert for five years.

Though she doesn't appear blond in photographs, this woman may have been Margery Pitt Durant. Margery was the daughter of automotive kingpin William Durant, who formed General Motors in 1908, created Chevrolet in 1910 and founded the Durant Car Company in 1921. Despite the restrictions on remarriage imposed by his divorce, Robert apparently went ahead and married Margery later in 1923.

Robert became a father on November 2, 1924, when Margery gave birth to their daughter in New York City. She was named Margery Randolph Daniel.

The Daniels purchased and restored the historic Virginia plantation Brandon in 1926. The property, located along the banks of the James River, has a history that dates to 1616. The main house was reportedly designed by Thomas Jefferson. Robert personally restored Brandon's famous stables, and he had the already expansive property enlarged further. The couple held lavish parties on the estate.

The Daniel family faithfully attended the local Episcopal church, located on what was originally part of the Brandon estate. It was alleged that Robert requested that the hymn "Nearer, My God, to Thee" never be played during a service in which he was in attendance, a claim recently verified by his daughter-in-law.

At Brandon, little Margery became accomplished as an equestrian and marksman. She attended St. Catherine's School in Richmond, where she

Titanic survivor Robert Williams Daniel (*second from left*) was aided in his political career by Virginia governor George C. Peery. *Library of Congress, Prints and Photographs Division.*

and four inseparable childhood friends would come to be known as the "Filthy Five."

As with his first, Robert's marriage to Margery ended in divorce. It was reported in July 1928 that Margery had established herself in Nevada—probably Reno—with the purpose of suing for divorce. Robert was by this time president of his father-in-law's Liberty National Bank in New York. William Durant referred to the situation as "one of those unfortunate matters that can't be helped." He noted that his business relations with Robert would "go on as usual."

Robert allegedly blamed his second divorce on a legend related to his plantation home dating back to when Benjamin Harrison lived there. Many years ago, so goes the tale, a bride who was wed beneath the large chandelier died suddenly on her wedding night. Her ring was embedded in the plaster ceiling by the chandelier, and it was said that whoever disturbed the ring would meet with romantic misfortune. While the house was being renovated in 1926, a portion of plaster fell to the floor, and the ring within was exposed. Robert cleaned and replaced it, but it was too late for his marriage to Margery.

A third marriage, to the widow Charlotte Williams Bemiss, came on October 10, 1929. Born on December 24, 1890, Charlotte was the daughter of Eli Lockert Bemiss and Cyane Williams Bemiss. She and Robert were distant cousins.

Robert, a Democrat, was elected to the Virginia Senate in 1935, representing the Sixth District. His tenure, beginning in 1936, would last four years.

On March 17, 1936, Charlotte gave birth to a son. The baby was named Robert Williams Daniel Jr.

Having struggled with alcoholism for a number of years, Robert Williams Daniel succumbed to cirrhosis of the liver on December 20, 1940. Fifty-six years old, he was laid to rest in an elegant crypt in the family plot in Hollywood Cemetery. Robert still held his seat in the Senate at the time of his death. His widow, Charlotte, would join him in the cemetery in 1968, dying on August 15 at the age of seventy-seven.

Robert Williams Daniel did not live to see his son and namesake become a successful and well-respected politician. Graduating from the University of Virginia in 1958, Robert Jr. worked for a time as a financial analyst, later teaching economics at the University of Richmond. He spent four years working for the Central Intelligence Agency. Robert Jr. served five terms in Congress representing Virginia's Fourth Congressional District. He died on February 4, 2012, at the age of seventy-five.

Daughter Margery lived to be eighty-eight years old, dying in May 2013. During World War II, she spent four years working for the Red Cross as a nurse's aide at McGuire Hospital and at the United States Army and Air Force base in Richmond. A fall from horseback in 1962 left her with a severe brain injury; yet, "after years of true grit, determination, and beating all odds," she fully recovered.

Like her father, Margery Randolph Daniel Merrick was a survivor.[44]

CANCELLED BOOKINGS

Mr. and Mrs. W.A. Fitzpatrick of Bedford, Virginia, had been touring Europe for several months in the spring of 1912. They returned home on Sunday, April 21, and quickly relayed to the local press the story of their near-brush with disaster. The couple claimed to have arrived in Liverpool, England, "just one day too late to catch the *Titanic*," though, they stated, the vessel they did return on took the same route and encountered stormy weather.[45]

It should be noted that no records of a booking for the name *Fitzpatrick* for *Titanic*'s maiden voyage are known to exist and that the ship departed from Southampton, not Liverpool. It could very well be that the couple had intended to book the new ship if they were able and that they arrived in Liverpool with their plan being to proceed to Southampton, had they arrived in time to make the maiden voyage. Their intentions might also have been exaggerated for the newspaper reporter, as this close call with tragedy made an excellent story for the local press.

Bessie Boley of Rockbridge, Virginia, at the time staying in Baltimore, Maryland, wrote to her friends at home following news of the disaster, informing them that she was going to have to make different travel arrangements. Boley had booked passage on the return leg of *Titanic*'s maiden voyage, intending to depart New York on April 20, 1912. She was able to secure passage onboard another ship, departing April 22.[46]

RMS *BALTIC*

During its maiden voyage, *Titanic* began receiving a series of ice warnings via its Marconi wireless set. On Sunday, April 14, 1912, the RMS *Baltic*, an older ship in the White Star Line's fleet, sent the following message to the *Titanic*:

> *Captain Smith,* Titanic—*Have had moderate, variable winds and clear, fine weather since leaving. Greek steamer* Athenai *reports passing icebergs and large quantities of field ice to-day in lat. 41° 51' N., long. 49° 52' W. Last night we spoke German oil tank steamer* Deutschland, *Stettin to Philadelphia, not under control, short of coal, lat. 40° 42' N., long. 55° 11' W. Wishes to be reported to New York and other steamers. Wish you and* Titanic *all success.—Commander.*[47]

Onboard the *Baltic* at that time were four "of Roanoke's most accomplished ladies." They were Elizabeth Ewart, sisters Lula and Lila Terry and Martha C. Wilson. The four socialites were traveling to Europe for a spring sojourn.[48] In the very early hours of April 15, 1912, the *Baltic* was one of the ships to receive *Titanic*'s distress call. From the Cunard Line's *Caronia*, the following message was relayed to *Baltic*'s Marconi operator: "MGY [*Titanic*] struck iceberg, requires immediate assistance."[49]

Baltic's captain then had the following reply sent to *Titanic* via *Caronia*: "Please tell *Titanic* we are making towards her."[50]

Four of Roanoke's most prominent socialites were aboard the *Baltic* when it received *Titanic*'s distress call. *Author's collection.*

The *Baltic*'s captain altered his course and steamed toward the ailing vessel, but unfortunately, he was too far away to render assistance. On learning that RMS *Carpathia* had aboard it all known survivors, the *Baltic* resumed its previous course.

The four socialites from Roanoke, Virginia, returned home on June 29, 1912. Once again, they traveled onboard the RMS *Baltic*.[51]

CHARLES MELVILLE HAYS

One reason why the story of the *Titanic* disaster is so enduring is the number of noted individuals traveling in first class who perished. One of these people was Charles Melville Hays, president of the Grand Trunk Railway in Canada. Surprisingly, a friend of this illustrious businessman visited Southwest Virginia in May 1912 and relayed some interesting stories about Hays.

Mr. G.F. Sullivan, representing F.S. Bowser & Co., of Fort Wayne, Ind., was a caller at this office on last Friday. Mr. Sullivan is an old railroad man, having spent five years with the Grand Trunk railroad in Canada.

Speaking of the former president of the Grand Trunk line, Mr. Charles M. Hays, who lost his life in the Titanic *disaster, Mr. Sullivan related some interesting stories of the time Mr. Hays, fresh from the Wabash railroad and full of enthusiasm as to the economic operation of the same, hit the Grand Trunk, and of the resulting revolution in the operation of that road—how, under the old regime, the checks and rolls were sent to the station agents for distribution, but after Mr. Hays took charge a pay car was sent out, with the result that 23,000 unclaimed checks were returned to the general office at the end of the run. As a sample of the inefficiency and uneconomical operation of the road before the advent of Mr. Hays, he related how hacks were furnished to take the clerks in the general office to and from work at the company's expense and at each little station*

A friend of Charles Hays, president of Canada's Grand Trunk Railway, visited Tazewell shortly after his death on the *Titanic. Wikimedia Commons.*

along the line three baggage men were employed—one as boss and the other two to carry the baggage to and from the trains—no trucks being furnished to handle baggage, as in these days.

Such mismanagement can hardly, in these days of strenuous railroading, be realized, let alone tolerated.[52]

THE WHITE GHOST OF DISASTER

A very early "moving picture" based on the sinking of the *Titanic*, called *The White Ghost of Disaster*, had begun playing in certain parts of Southwest Virginia by August 1912, just four months after the tragedy. Three full reels, comprising three thousand feet of film, featured dramatic re-creations of the captivating disaster. The film played at Amuzu Theatre in Big Stone Gap in August 1912[53] and at the Silent Players Theatre in Salem two years later, on September 1, 1914.[54]

The White Ghost of Disaster played in Salem in September 1914. *Author's collection.*

ARTHUR EDWARD TRIPP

In mid-February 1914, a Salem, Virginia girl named Bessie Wiley "pleasantly surprised" her friends when she announced that she had gotten married at her mother's home the previous Thursday. The groom was named Arthur Edward Tripp, of Waterbury, Connecticut. The news became juicier when it was revealed that Arthur, a "promising young man" who worked as a draftsman, had survived the sinking of the *Titanic* two years earlier while returning home from a trip abroad in connection with his work.[55]

The unfortunate truth is that there was no Arthur Edward Tripp on board the *Titanic*. His name does not appear in connection with the maiden voyage in any way whatsoever. Also, despite extensive searching, I could locate no records relating to the marriage described in the 1914 article. What are we to make of this story? Did Arthur simply spin a yarn to impress Bessie or perhaps to obtain her pity? Was the added detail about the *Titanic* disaster some form of inside joke between the couple, or was it even an outright invention by an imaginative reporter? At this time, the available historical record simply does not answer these questions, but the story is certainly curious.

"THE SINKING OF THE *TITANIC*"

On State Street in Bristol, Tennessee, just around the corner from the Burger Bar, there is a small plaque mounted to a rock. Passersby would be forgiven for not even noticing the undistinguished monument. But on its face, an interesting bit of local history is recounted. As it turns out, a song written about the *Titanic* by an early country music artist from Southwest Virginia led to the famous Bristol Sessions. The plaque reads:

> *In 1924, Ernest V. "Pop" Stoneman (1893–1968) of Galax, Va., first recorded his self-penned song, "The Sinking of the* Titanic*", in New York for Ralph Peer at Okeh Records. It was his early commercial and financial success that first lured Ralph Peer, the Victor Talking Machine Company, and talented mountain musicians to the historic, 1927 "Bristol Sessions". Mr. Peer began the recording sessions with his star, Ernest V. Stoneman and his "Dixie Mountaineers", consisting of his wife, Hattie Frost "Mom" Stoneman (1900–1976), with friends and relatives.*

In 1924, Ernest V. "Pop" Stoneman (1893-1968) of Galax, Va., first recorded his self-penned song, "The Sinking of the Titanic", in New York for Ralph Peer at Okeh Records. It was his early commercial and financial success that lured Ralph Peer, the Victor Talking Machine Company, and many talented mountain musicians to the historic, 1927 "Bristol Sessions". Mr. Peer began the recording sessions with his star, Ernest V. Stoneman and his "Dixie Mountaineers", consisting of his wife, Hattie Frost "Mom" Stoneman (1900-1976), with friends and relatives.

• Using various names, "Pop" Stoneman recorded for 24 record labels. In 1928, because there were so many family members, he named the band, the "Stoneman Family".

According to the Library of Congress, Hattie "Mom" Stoneman was to become the first woman of importance in Country Music.

The Stoneman Family was awarded the first C.M.A. "Vocal Group of the Year", in 1967, with their father. The Smithsonian Institution, The Library of Congress and the B.C.M.A. have also honored them.

Fifteen of their children, Eddie, Grace, John, Patsy, Nita, Billy, Jack, Gene, Dean, Scott, Donna, Jimmy, Rita, Roni, and Van were to continue the musical heritage and legacy left them by their parents, making the Stoneman name the longest continuously active name in Country Music.

This plaque on State Street in Bristol commemorates the recording of the song "The Sinking of the *Titanic*" by Ernest V. Stoneman. *Author's collection.*

Using various names, "Pop" Stoneman recorded for 24 record labels. In 1928, because there were so many family members, he named the band, the "Stoneman Family".

According to the Library of Congress, Hattie "Mom" Stoneman was to become the first woman of importance in Country Music.

The Stoneman Family was awarded the first C.M.A. "Vocal Group of the Year", in 1967, with their father. The Smithsonian Institution, The Library of Congress and the B.C.M.A. have also honored them.

Fifteen of their children, Eddie, Grace, John, Patsy, Nita, Billy, Jack, Gene, Dean, Scott, Donna, Jimmy, Rita, Roni, and Van were to continue the musical heritage and legacy left them by their parents, making the Stoneman name the longest continuously active name in Country Music.

4

USS *MOUNT VERNON*

PAUL HOMER CROCKETT

Paul Homer Crockett was born on August 8, 1893, in Raven, Virginia. He was the son of John Isaac Crockett and his first wife, Cynthia A.J. Dickenson. An older sister, Margaret, had been born on July 26, 1879, and an older brother, William Gratton, had come into the world on August 27, 1887. A younger sister, Katherine, would be born on June 20, 1896.

The Crockett family appears to have been wealthy in acreage in the Raven area. On April 16, 1907, a condemnation announcement from the Norfolk & Western Railway Company, which was planning to run rails through part of the family's land, was given to the Crocketts. The announcement was printed in the local newspaper.

> *To condemn land under Virginia Code Section 1105f Sub-Sections 4 and 5, Pollard's Code 1904, pages 581–582.*
>
> *To James C. Dickenson, John I. Crockett, Margaret Gillespie (nee Crockett), J. Sam Gillespie her husband, Corrie Gillespie (nee Crockett), William Gillespie her husband, Dora Crockett, Kate Crockett, Paul Crockett and James Crockett, and to all whom it may concern:*
>
> *You are hereby notified that the Norfolk & Western Railway Company will on the 27th day of May, in the year 1907, that being the first day of the May 1907 term of the Circuit Court of Tazewell County, apply to the Circuit Court for the County of Tazewell, at the Courthouse of said*

County, for the appointment of Commissioners to ascertain what will be a just compensation for the fee simple interest or estate in a certain parcel of land which you own, or in which you are interested, which is proposed to be condemned for the uses and purposes of said Company, and to award the damages, if any, resulting to the adjacent and other property of the owner, or to the property of any other person, beyond the peculiar benefits that will accrue to said properties respectively from the construction and operation of the works of said Company.

The parcel of land above referred to contains 0.46 acre of land more or less, and is situated on the Coal Creek, a tributary of Clinch River, in Tazewell County, Virginia, and is a part of the 34¼ acres of land mentioned and described in deed of conveyance from said James C. Dickenson to John I. Crockett, bearing date September 28, 1898 and recorded in Tazewell County, in Deed Book 42, page 40, wherein and whereby the said J.C. Dickenson reserved a life estate unto himself, and conveyed to the said John I. Crockett, a contingent life estate, with remainder in fee simple to the children of Cynthia J. Crockett, deceased, and the said John I. Crockett her husband, living at the time of the death of the said John I. Crockett, and the issue of children dying per stirpes.

Parcel of land is more fully described on Plat of survey and profile showing cuts and fills, trestles and bridges, and in the petition for the appointment of Commissioners this day filed in the Clerk's Office of the Circuit Court of Tazewell County, Virginia, by the undersigned, stating the material facts upon which application is based.

NORFOLK & WESTERN RAILWAY CO.,
By Henry & Graham and S.D. May, Attorneys.
April 16, 1907.[56]

John Isaac Crockett had made the local newspaper several times over the years. On June 13, 1912, he gave an exhibition of his new automobile in town. This would have attracted a great deal of attention in an era when car ownership was still rare, particularly in rural areas.[57]

In June 1915, John announced his intention to run for supervisor of the Maiden Spring district.[58] He ultimately lost the election that November to W.L.C. Burke, garnering only 92 votes to Burke's 411. In second place came D.C. Lowe, with 385 votes.[59]

On November 29, 1917, Sam Gillespie sent a note to the local newspaper exclaiming the incredible size of John Crockett's hogs: "Mr. John I. Crockett,

Firemen are shown at work in USS *Mount Vernon*'s No. 4 boiler room. Paul Homer Crockett served in this same role. *Naval History and Heritage Command.*

of this city, killed two hogs Tuesday, which net him 1,390 pounds, one of them was a three-year-old and the other was 19 months old. They were about, according to my judgment, 790 and 600."[60]

When the United States entered World War I on April 6, 1917, Paul Homer Crockett was twenty-three years old. Soon after President Woodrow Wilson's declaration of war, Paul traveled to Parkersburg, West Virginia, where he enlisted in the U.S. Navy on May 17, 1917.

September 1918 saw this local hero serving aboard the troop transport USS *Mount Vernon* in the capacity of fireman second class. Formerly the luxurious German passenger ship SS *Kronprinzessin Cecilie*, the vessel was interned in Bar Harbor, Maine, at the outbreak of hostilities in 1914, later rechristened as a transport vessel for the United States. This followed a futile attempt by the German crew to disguise the ship as the White Star Line's famous *Olympic*. As a fireman, Paul would have spent his on-duty hours in the ship's sweltering boiler rooms, shoveling coal into the furnaces. The manual labor was intensive, the sweltering heat of the fireroom brutal.

SS *Kronprinzessin Cecilie* shortly after internment, before its rechristening as USS *Mount Vernon* by the U.S. Navy. *Naval History and Heritage Command.*

On September 5, 1918, the *Mount Vernon*, under the command of Captain Desmond E. Dismukes, was sailing in a convoy from Brest, France, to New York. Approximately 250 miles off the coast of France, the German submarine *U-82* was sighted. Though the *Vernon*'s crew took evasive measures and fired at the submarine, *U-82* successfully launched a torpedo. *Mount Vernon* was struck amidships, in the location of the ship's boiler rooms.

At the moment of impact, Homer Crockett was on duty in Boiler Room No. 4.[61] It is likely that he was killed instantly by the torpedo's detonation. In total, thirty-six members of the *Vernon*'s engineering staff died in the attack, and an additional twelve were injured. As the wounded ship steamed away under the cover of a smokescreen, the dead remained in the instantly flooded boiler room, from which they would later be recovered. Despite the damage incurred, the *Mount Vernon* remained afloat and was later repaired in a dry dock in Brest and afterward resumed its wartime duties.

News of Homer's untimely death at sea would not break in his rural hometown's newspaper, the *Clinch Valley News*, until one week later, on September 13.

USS *Mount Vernon* being escorted just after the torpedo attack. It is surrounded by a smokescreen. *Naval History and Heritage Command.*

In the weeks following, John I. Crockett received a number of letters of condolence from high-ranking naval officials. Rear Admiral H.B. Wilson wrote the following from Brest, France, on September 9, 1918:

> *Word has already been sent you of the death of your son, Paul Homer Crockett, but I wish to add the expression of my most sincere sympathy.*
>
> *When his ship was attacked and torpedoed by an enemy submarine, your son bravely made the supreme sacrifice for his country, by giving his life in the performance of his duty. Death is always sad, but there is something splendid in a man's sacrificing himself for the cause of his country.*
>
> *A service was held today with full military honors. Mr. Franklin Roosevelt, the Assistant Secretary of the Navy, attended with me, as well as a large representation of officers and men. The French Admiral was present with a number of officers and men of the French Navy.*[62]

On September 11, 1918, *Mount Vernon*'s Captain Dismukes wrote from the damaged vessel:

> *U.S.S.* Mount Vernon, *11 September, 1918.*
> *Mr. John I. Crockett, Raven, Va.*
>
> *My Dear Sir: You were, no doubt, promptly informed by the Navy Department of the unfortunate death of your son Paul, who lost his life while the U.S.S.* Mount Vernon *was in battle with an enemy submarine on the morning of 5 September, 1918.*
>
> *It is with deep sorrow, mingled with unbounded pride that I write you of your noble sacrifice. He died as a brave man should in these times—at his post of duty in the service of his country.*
>
> *The ship was struck by a torpedo which exploded in the fireroom where he was on duty. He, with thirty-five other men, was killed and twelve wounded. He was either killed outright by the explosion or instantly drowned by the enormous inrush of water through the hole made by the torpedo. He was a member of the finest engineers force it has ever been my pleasure to be associated with and it was due to the gallant conduct of those who survive that the ship was brought safely into port.*
>
> *His remains have been shipped home to you and should arrive soon after this letter. His effects, which were carefully inventoried by his Division Officer, should arrive at the same time.*

Permit me to express the deepest sympathy for you in behalf of myself and the Mount Vernon's *entire crew. We deem it an honor to have served with your noble son.*

Yours most respectfully,
D.E. DISMUKES,
Captain, U.S. Navy, commanding.[63]

Accompanying the correspondence received by Mr. Crockett were copies of several special orders issued by commanding officers of the navy. The following note was attached to Special Order No. 3, dated September 8, 1918, from Secretary of War Newton D. Baker:

My Dear Captain Dismukes:

I have been so moved by the splendid conduct of the officers and men who saved the Mount Vernon *that I have cabled the Secretary of the Navy and I enclose a copy of its message in the hope that its expressions may convey to you, your officers and your men some sense of the pride our country will feel in this story of courage, loyalty, and successful daring.*

With your lost comrades, you who have been mercifully saved have added another page to the Navy's best traditions and I wish you all, my late shipmates, continued success and all good fortune in the great cause you have so nobly served.

Cordially yours,
NEWTON D. BAKER,
Cablegram.[64]

Secretary Baker had visited the *Mount Vernon* soon after the torpedoing and issued a glowing cablegram to Washington:

For Secretary of Navy, Washington. I have just visited and viewed the Mount Vernon. *The high spirited morale of its men and the masterful seamanship of its captain and officers makes a stirring story of heroism that I wish all the Nation might know the splendid way in which that huge transport met and foiled the attempt to destroy it at sea. The traditions of your service are enriched by the conduct of this emergency.*

NEWTON D. BAKER,
Secretary of War.[65]

Captain Desmond E. Dismukes, USN, was commanding officer of the USS *Mount Vernon*. *Naval History and Heritage Command.*

This previously unpublished image shows workmen in the dry dock in Brest, France, repairing *Mount Vernon*'s torpedo damage. *Author's collection.*

Above: Secretary of the Navy Josephus Daniels is firing a boiler on the USS *Mount Vernon* while a group of firemen, one of whom might be Paul Homer Crockett, looks on with amusement. *The Woodrow Wilson Presidential Library & Museum.*

Left: Paul Homer Crockett's grave marker in Clinch Valley Memorial Cemetery, Richlands, recalls his death at sea. *Author's collection.*

The bodies of the lost were sent home in flag-draped coffins for burial in U.S. soil. Paul's body would have reached his home by train, probably being unloaded at the long-gone train depot in Raven or possibly the one in Richlands. The bodies were escorted across the ocean by a future president, Assistant Secretary of the Navy Franklin D. Roosevelt.

Following the end of World War I on November 11, 1918, Paul's name appeared on the "Roll Call of the Dead" alongside those of twenty-six other young men from Tazewell County, Virginia, who were killed during the war.[66]

John Isaac Crockett appears to have remained active in his community following the loss of his son at sea. On December 22, 1922, he was described as having made an "excellent" Santa Claus for the Pisgah School.[67]

Paul Homer Crockett, age twenty-five, now rests in Clinch Valley Memorial Cemetery in Richlands, Virginia, alongside his parents and other family members. Their graves are located on the sloping hillside to the right of the mausoleum. Paul was originally interred near the family home in Raven in late September 1918, accompanied by a band of sailors,[68] as the Clinch Valley Memorial Cemetery was not established until 1938.

Paul's marker makes note of his death on the USS *Mount Vernon* so that all who pass his grave may know of the ultimate sacrifice this young man made.

5

SS *VESTRIS*

It is likely that no famous sea tragedy has a closer connection to Southwest Virginia than the 1928 sinking of the SS *Vestris*. On November 12, foundering under heavy weather and the negligent overloading of its cargo holds, the *Vestris* sank approximately two hundred miles off the coast of Virginia with the loss of 117 passengers and crew, including all 13 children onboard.[69] Today relegated to a minor footnote in maritime history, in the vessel's own time, its sinking and the resulting loss of life made headlines in a manner similar to the sinkings of the *Titanic* and *Lusitania* in their times.

For a number of the 210 survivors, their ordeal did not end on November 12. On December 10, 1928, while carrying 25 of the *Vestris*'s survivors, the White Star Line's RMS *Celtic* ran aground on the rocks at Roche's Point off Cobh, Ireland.

Among the first-class passengers were four people who called Southwest Virginia home, all of whom lost their lives in the sinking: a family of missionaries from Abingdon and a young engineer from Christiansburg. These are their stories.

ERNEST ALONZO, JANNETTE AND CARY JACKSON

Nestled within the Appalachian Mountains in Southwest Virginia is the picturesque town of Abingdon. Known primarily as the location of the historic Barter Theatre, where stars such as Ernest Borgnine and Gregory

RMS *Celtic* met its own demise with a number of survivors of the *Vestris* on board. *Author's collection.*

Peck cut their acting teeth, this town also holds a link to a noted maritime tragedy, a link that until recently I was completely unaware of.

On a corner across the street from the Barter, within earshot of the murmur of theatergoers, stands a lovely three-story brick home with an elaborate front porch of white-painted wood. Few if any passersby strolling Abingdon's brick sidewalks would have ever heard of a lost ship called the *Vestris* or realize that the house at 102 East Main Street was once the home of three of its victims. But in 1928, this was the residence of the Jacksons, a family once well known in the small town.

Ernest Alonzo Jackson was born on August 13, 1877, in the early nineteenth-century plantation house known as Brook Hall in Glade Spring, Virginia. His mother, Mary Cloyd Ernest, had been born there also, on January 7, 1850. Ernest's father, Stephen Alonzo Jackson, was born on September 22, 1851, in Glenville, West Virginia.[70] While attending the University of Virginia, Stephen played a significant role in the establishment of the Sigma Kappa fraternity, and he remains a somewhat legendary figure in the organization's history to this day. He died at the age of forty on March 4, 1892, and was buried in Abingdon's Sinking Spring Cemetery. The centenary of Stephen Alonzo Jackson's death was commemorated in Charlottesville and Abingdon, Virginia, on March 7–8, 1992, with Centennial Jackson Day.

The former residence of the Jackson family stands on Main Street in Abingdon. *Author's collection.*

The widowed Mary Ernest Jackson was remarried to Thomas Dobie Davidson on November 12, 1898. Davidson was a Princeton University graduate, Civil War veteran and former president of the Stonewall Jackson Institute. That school for girls, located in Abingdon, would eventually become Stonewall Jackson College and remain in operation until 1930. Nearly twenty-five years his new wife's senior, Davidson would die ten years later on August 13, 1908, in Wytheville, Virginia.

Ernest Alonzo, commonly referred to as E.A., attended Roanoke College and Emory & Henry College. On December 31, 1902, E.A. married Jannette Beazley in the Mt. Zion Baptist Church in Dunbrooke, Virginia. Born on September 3, 1870, in Essex County, Virginia, Jannette attended the Mission Training Institute in Nyack, New York, alongside her new husband.

On January 1, 1903, immediately following their marriage, the Jacksons were appointed by the Foreign Mission Board of Southern Baptist Convention to begin missionary work in South America. On February 20, the couple sailed for Bahia, Brazil, on their first mission trip. A newspaper noted that Brother Jackson had sailed to Brazil several years earlier as part of the Christian Alliance and that he was a Presbyterian at that time. "On close study of God's word he became a Baptist in faith," himself being baptized by the Reverend Z.C. Taylor. "He has already done a fine work in Brazil."[71]

In November 1903, Jannette gave birth to twins while residing in Santa Rita de Rio Preto, Bahia, Brazil. The newborn girls were named Earnestine Beazley and Mary Catherine Jackson. Sadly, the babies would live less than three months. Mary Catherine died on January 24, 1904, and Earnestine followed two days later.

Six more children would follow, four sons and two daughters. With the exception of daughter Virginia Frances, who was born in Abingdon during a visit home, all of E A. and Jannette's children were born in South American locales. Elizabeth Byars arrived on December 25, 1904; James Earnest on April 8, 1906; Judson Gordon on January 31, 1908; Virginia Frances on May 13, 1909; Stephen Pomeroy on February 27, 1911; and the youngest, Cary Boughan, was born on November 1, 1913.[72]

When home on furlough from their missionary work, Reverend Jackson and his growing family generally stayed at the home of his elderly mother on Main Street in Abingdon. Following an extended stay in the United States in 1923, E.A. reapplied for a passport in the U.S. District Court of Abingdon, Virginia. In the application, he was recorded as standing five feet, eight inches tall, with black hair, brown eyes, a smooth face and a ruddy complexion.[73]

By 1928, five of the Jacksons' six children were grown and several were noted to be attending school in Tennessee. Late that fall, E.A., Jannette and newly turned fifteen-year-old Cary paid them a visit. They undoubtedly also visited the elderly Mrs. Jackson in Abingdon for what would prove to be the final time.

On Saturday, November 10, 1928, the Lamport and Holt steamer *Vestris* departed Pier 14 in Hoboken, New Jersey, bound for Rio de Janeiro, Montevideo and Buenos Aires. Aboard in first class, returning to their missionary work in Brazil, were E.A., Jannette and Cary. The previous year, the family had traveled on the *Vestris*'s sister, the *Vandyck*, and E.A.'s travel history with the Lamport and Holt Line extended as far back as 1899.

Ernest Alonzo Jackson is shown here in his younger years, likely at the beginning of his missionary work. *Southern Baptist Historical Library & Archives.*

On Saturday, while on board the *Vestris*, E.A. wrote a letter to the Reverend Leland Smith of Central Baptist Church in Fountain City, Tennessee. It was received on November 13. The reverend then showed it to groups gathered at the State Baptist Convention at the First Baptist Church the following day, as the sinking of the *Vestris* was by then a topic of great discussion. In his letter, E.A. told how he had enjoyed his recent furlough in Knoxville, during which time he was said to have filled pulpits, and he mentioned his appreciation of the friendship between he and Smith. "We had a most pleasant trip to New York," E.A. wrote in closing. "I have great hopes for the work here and abroad." No mention was made of any trouble with the ship, though Smith noted that the letter was penned in an angular hand, with some of the letters appearing much darker than the others. He thought this might have been caused by the lurching of the ship.[74]

Exemplary of their Christian faith, as the tragedy unfolded on November 12, the Jacksons were seen in the first-class smoking room handing out life jackets to their fellow passengers before leading the gathered group in prayer, invoking God to guide them safely through their mounting predicament.[75]

While a number of passengers were likely saved in part because of their selfless actions, Ernest Alonzo, Jannette and Cary lost their lives in the sinking. Their bodies were not identified as being among the twenty-two recovered from the sea. It is sad that the selfless heroics of the Jacksons never entered the canon of timeless sea stories alongside the inseparable Strauses of the *Titanic* or the chivalrous Alfred Gwynne Vanderbilt of the *Lusitania*.

By November 17, it was being reported that hope for the Jacksons had been given up. The *Bristol Herald Courier* reported that a telegram had been received from Dr. Thomas F. Staley, of Bristol, a cousin of the Jacksons who had been in New York for several days, stating that he had just returned from Staten Island, where he had personally examined twenty unidentified bodies of *Vestris* victims, but that the Jacksons were not among them.[76]

Two of the Jacksons' children, Judson and Virginia, then students at the University of Tennessee, continued to cling to hope that their parents and little brother had survived the disaster. It was reported that the two siblings were "bearing up bravely and awaiting definite news of the fate of their missing parents and brother."[77]

The *Knoxville Journal* on November 17 painted a touching word-picture of the grief expressed by Judson Jackson:

> *The tragedy of the* Vestris *has seemed very near and very real to* The Journal *staff this week. For three nights a pale-faced young man has come to the editorial office and asked: "Any news of the Jacksons yet?" And for three nights the editors have been compelled to answer: "They are still listed as missing."*
>
> *The young man is Judson Jackson, son of the Rev. and Mrs. E.A. Jackson, Baptist missionaries, who with their young son, Cary, were lost on the* Vestris.
>
> The Journal *staff, accustomed to viewing tragedy, extends to young Judson Jackson its sincere admiration as well as its heartfelt sympathy. For he is one of the bravest young men we have ever seen.*
>
> *Night after night he has scanned eagerly the sheaf of dispatches on the telegraph editor's desk, hoping against hope for some ray of encouragement.*

Left: This stunning photograph was taken on November 12, 1928, from the Boat Deck of the *Vestris*. Passengers and crew desperately struggle with the portside lifeboats against the ship's dangerous list to starboard. *Library of Congress, Prints and Photographs Division.*

Below: This 1919 view of the *Vestris* shows the ship listing heavily to port after a fire in one of the holds was extinguished. *Author's collection.*

Each dispatch has been more ominously hopeless, but young Judson has not winced or complained. He has read the dispatches stoically, and gone bravely away, only to reappear later with the familiar question: "Any news yet?"

We have almost ached to give him some good news, but there was none. We doff our hats to him as one who has stood erect with dignity beneath as crushing a load of sorrow as can come to a mortal.[78]

At 3:00 p.m. on December 9, 1928, nearly one month after they were lost at sea, a memorial service for the Jacksons was held in the Abingdon Baptist Church. Reverend F.M. Huggins, pastor of the church, was in charge of the services. The service was said to have been well attended. E.A.'s mother had remained a Presbyterian, and her pastor, Reverend J.G. Patton, opened the service with prayer followed by the reading of Psalm 91.

The Baptist choir then sang "Abide with Me," followed by a recitation of the life of Reverend Jackson by Reverend Huggins. The choir then sang "In the Hour of Trial." Following that hymn, Reverend G.A. Maiden, pastor of the Abingdon Methodist Church, made what were said to be "very touching" remarks about the family, after which the choir of the Stonewall Jackson College sang "Lead Kindly Light."[79]

The service continued with several noted speakers. Summaries of their remarks were recorded by the local press:

Dr. Thomas F. Staley, of Bristol, lifelong friend and kinsman of Rev. Jackson, gave a beautiful eulogy and tribute to his boyhood friend and cousin.

Dr. Denton, friend and medical advisor, recounted miracle after miracle which Rev. Jackson had told him had come to him in answer to prayer and faith.

Mr. Copenhaver, of Seven Mile Ford, told of the benediction and influence of Rev. and Mrs. Jackson's and Cary's visit to his family shortly before the Jacksons sailed on their final voyage.

The pastor of the colored Baptist Church of Abingdon, Rev. Brown spoke of the wonderful influence Rev. Jackson had over his congregation, always speaking to them whenever he visited Abingdon and enlisting their interest in the great field of world-wide missions, also deepening and enriching the spiritual life of those with whom he came in contact and to whom he preached.[80]

The lengthy memorial service closed with Reverend Huggins reading "Crossing the Bar," which was said to have been the favorite poem of the Jacksons. The choir concluded the service by singing "Saved by His Grace," said to have been one of the family's favorite hymns.[81]

Mary Ernest Davidson was devastated by her simultaneous losses, and sometime after the *Vestris* disaster she moved away from Abingdon. Mary spent her final days in Radford, Virginia, where she died on July 9, 1937, at the age of eighty-seven. Her body was returned to Abingdon, where she was interred beside her first husband in Sinking Spring Cemetery. She was buried under the last name Davidson. There is no mention of the *Vestris* at their gravesite.

As they grew older, the five remaining Jackson children scattered throughout the United States. When daughter Elizabeth Byars died on December 3, 1999, at the age of ninety-four, her ashes were scattered at sea over the location where the *Vestris* is believed to have gone down, taking her parents and younger brother with it. Son Stephen Pomeroy Jackson became a second-generation Brazilian missionary. He died on July 29, 1996, and his headstone in Texas memorializes his family lost at sea, though the date of the disaster is given incorrectly as November 10. The

USS *Wyoming* came to the aid of the *Vestris*'s survivors. *Naval History and Heritage Command.*

last surviving child, Judson Gordon Jackson, passed away on February 9, 2005, at the age of ninety-seven.[82]

In present-day Abingdon, no memorial to the town's *Vestris* victims is to be found. It is likely that 99 percent of the locals have never even heard of the shipwreck, or of Ernest Alonzo, Jannette and Cary Jackson. Yet the family's imprint is still present. The former Jackson home on Main Street remains in pristine condition, proudly standing within Abingdon's historic district. The town library was founded by Mary Ernest Jackson when she began loaning books from the ground floor of her home. Today, the Washington County Public Library System consists of the main Abingdon location, as well as four branches. In nearby Glade Spring, Brook Hall remains standing, a private residence and historical point of interest.

CHARLES INGLES WADE STONE

The fourth link to our region on the *Vestris*'s fateful final voyage was a young man from Christiansburg, Virginia, named Charles Ingles Wade Stone. Charles was born in Christiansburg, Montgomery County, on March 27, 1898. His father was Henry Thomas Stone, a traveling salesman, born on November 7, 1866. Henry married Charles's mother, music teacher Mary Lynn Wade, on November 29, 1894. Born on May 27, 1868, Mary was noted for her singing voice. On June 16, 1906, she served as an accompanist in a performance of Frederic Comer's cantata "The Rose Maiden" in Radford, Virginia.[83]

Henry and Mary had six children, three boys and three girls. A baby daughter, Margaret Alan Stone, sadly died on July 24, 1900, after only four months of life. Another daughter, Agnes McClanahan Stephens, died on August 6, 1924, at the age of twenty-three. Of the girls, only the third daughter, Frances Roedel, lived to see old age. She lived to age sixty-seven, dying on April 15, 1972.

Charles was named after a maternal uncle, Charles Ingles Wade. A prominent citizen of Christiansburg, the elder Charles was one of the founders of the Bank of Christiansburg, and he served as the treasurer of the Virginia Mechanical and Agricultural College, a branch of the Virginia Polytechnic Institute, from 1895 until his death on April 6, 1935.

After graduating from Christiansburg High School, Charles I.W. Stone followed what appears to have been something of a family tradition, enrolling at Virginia Polytechnic Institute, known commonly today as

Charles Stone (*seated, second from left in the front row*) is seen in this 1919 group portrait of VPI's Maury Literary Society. The Bugle, *1919 edition, Special Collections and University Archives, University Libraries, Virginia Polytechnic Institute and State University.*

Virginia Tech. His two brothers, Thomas Henry Stone Jr. and John Allen Stone, had both graduated from the institute. In fact, John would go on to serve as the college's president. Located in Blacksburg, Virginia, the institute made international news when, on April 16, 2007, a crazed gunman heinously killed thirty-two students and faculty members in the deadliest school shooting in the nation's history.

Charles entered Virginia Polytechnic Institute as a freshman in 1916, his course of study being electrical engineering. By 1918, he was a junior. In the 1919 edition of the college's yearbook, *The Bugle*, Charles is shown as having served as vice-president of the Maury Literary Society, and he is listed as a corporal in Company B of the Students' Army Training Corps (SATC). The yearbook says this about the activities of the SATC: "Although all activities received a severe setback on account of the epidemic of Spanish influenza, the Corps progressed rapidly and preparations were being made for the transfer of the first quota to Officers' Training Camps when the armistice was signed. The cessation of hostilities sounded the death knell of the Students' Army Training Corps. It passed away as quickly and efficiently as it had arisen."[84]

On September 12, 1918, just two months before the cessation of hostilities, Charles registered for the draft. He listed his occupation at that time as "electrician helper" and his employer as E.I. DuPont de Nemours and Company. Charles gave his address as 507 North 3½ Street in Hopewell, Virginia.[85] These details strongly suggest that by the time of his draft registration, Charles was no longer a student, and *The Bugle* does not list him as a member of the graduating class for 1920. From what can be ascertained by existing records, he did not see active military duty. For some time, he was employed by the college's treasurer's office as an assistant.

By 1927, Charles had relocated from Southwest Virginia to New York, where he was employed as an accountant for the foundational engineering firm Dwight P. Robinson and Company. His brother Henry also worked for the company, as a purchaser.[86]

In the fall of 1928, Charles was assigned to travel to Rio de Janeiro as part of a new South American project the company was undertaking. He dutifully booked a first-class passage for himself on the *Vestris*, departing from New

Charles Stone served as a corporal in Company B of VPI's Student's Army Training Corps, here seen in 1919. The Bugle, *1919 edition, Special Collections and University Archives, University Libraries, Virginia Polytechnic Institute and State University.*

York Harbor on November 10. Having just traveled back to New York from a job in Chicago, this "young man of affable personality"[87] took the time to make a long-distance telephone call to his parents in Christiansburg before boarding the ship. It was the last time they would ever speak. His last known visit to Christiansburg was for Christmas in 1927.[88]

Charles Ingles Wade Stone's movements throughout the brief, chaotic final voyage of the *Vestris* are not known. With only sixty-two passengers booked in first class, it is quite possible that some time during the voyage he met fellow Southwest Virginia travelers Ernest Alonzo, Jannette and Cary Jackson.

The *Vestris* disappeared beneath the choppy, gray waves at approximately 2:00 p.m. on November 12, 1928, taking Charles with it. His body was not identified as being one of the few recovered from the sea. He was only thirty years old.

Virginia Polytechnic Institute's 1929 Alumni Register, the first to be published after 1920, has the following sparse notation: "Stone, Chas. I.W., '20, Elec. Eng., Deceased."[89]

FIRST-CLASS DINING SALOON.

The four *Vestris* passengers from Southwest Virginia would have taken their meals here, in the first-class dining saloon. *Author's collection.*

A stern view of the listing *Vestris*, taken soon after the ship was evacuated during the 1919 fire. *Author's collection.*

In 1938, at the tenth anniversary of the sinking, Charles's name was mentioned again in the press in connection with the tragedy that ended his life. It was stated mournfully that he "had the promise of a splendid future." It was noted that his mother, Mary, was paid $1,935.35 in compensation for the loss of her son.[90]

Henry Thomas Stone lived to age seventy-three, passing away on September 6, 1940, of an intracranial hemorrhage suffered after a fall down stairs. Mary Lynn Wade Stone lived to age eighty-six, her life ending on February 21, 1955. The entire family is buried together in Sunset Cemetery in Christiansburg. Yet there is no cenotaph or any known memorial to Charles Ingles Wade Stone. Even more so than the *Vestris* itself, those who sailed and died aboard it on that tragic day are rarely, if ever, recalled.

6

SS MORRO CASTLE

On September 8, 1934, a fire broke out aboard the American ocean liner SS *Morro Castle*, en route from Hoboken, New Jersey, to Havana, Cuba. In the end, 128 people were either confirmed dead or listed as missing, ranking the vessel high on lists of infamous ships of history.[91] Though now recalled primarily by old-timers in the Asbury Park area of New Jersey, where the burning hulk of the ship came to rest and temporarily became a macabre tourist attraction, with many photographs being taken of it in situ and sold as souvenir postcards, the fire was a major news story at the time.

The tragedy aboard the *Morro Castle* has all the mysterious plot twists of a thriller novel. Earlier in the evening on September 7, after complaining of abdominal pain, Captain Robert Renison Willmott was found dead in his cabin of what was believed to have been a heart attack. The comparatively inexperienced chief officer, William Warms, then took over command, just as the *astle* steamed toward a forceful nor'easter. Hours later, a fire was found to be raging inside the ship, the conflagration fanned by the strong winds. To top it off, one of the vessel's radio operators, George Rogers, was a highly suspicious individual, later found guilty of murdering his elderly neighbors. Many conspiratorial fingers have pointed toward Rogers—or even a hypothetical undercover Cuban agent—as the true reason behind the fire and possibly the captain's untimely death. A more down-to-earth and technical explanation for the fire, involving the overheating of the casing around one of the ship's funnels, has also been put forth. In the end, the exact cause of the loss of the *Morro Castle* remains an unusual and intriguing mystery of the sea.

Postmarked from Cuba in 1930, this pre-disaster postcard portrays the *Morro Castle* in happier days. *Author's collection.*

HARRY ACREE LIPSCOMB

Southwest Virginia had one known connection to the SS *Morro Castle*. His name was Harry Acree Lipscomb. Born on September 11, 1884, to Charles Patterson and Susan Pauline Wray Lipscomb, Harry was two days shy of his fiftieth birthday when he perished at sea. Originally from Lynchburg, Virginia, he had been living for some time in Alexandria, where he was a long-term employee of the Southern Railway, for which he served as a yard conductor at the time of his death.[92]

Much of the information about Lipscomb that is contained in this narrative was kindly provided by his granddaughter Sandra Holt. Harry Acree Lipscomb was her mother's father. Though often misspelled, per Sandra's maternal family, there should be no "e" on the end of Lipscomb, and the name is properly pronounced "lips-come."

Sandra has been told that her grandfather was quite the "dandy" and that he greatly enjoyed his work with the other employees of the railway. Though Sandra was never quite certain what was meant by calling him a "dandy," her grandfather appears to have always been sharply dressed; in every photograph Sandra has seen of him, Harry is "dressed to the nines."[93]

Harry was married to Mary Ellen Williams sometime in the years before World War I. The couple would eventually have five children, three daughters and two sons.

Lipscomb registered for the draft on September 9, 1918. He was thirty-three years old. At that time, he gave his address as 719 Gibbon Street in Alexandria. He listed his occupation as railroad conductor. His eyes were noted as being brown and his hair color black, and he was marked as being medium in both height and build.[94]

A few years before Harry's untimely death, some conflict occurred that broke the family apart. Sandra was never told what took place or if her grandfather and grandmother were actually divorced or merely separated after the break. Sandra stated that her grandmother was a "strict Catholic," so for her, a divorce may have been out of the question.

Following the mysterious event that turned his family on end, Harry brought Sandra's mother from Alexandria to Lynchburg to be cared for and schooled but did not bring his other children. Why he showed such favoritism to this daughter remains another mystery.[95]

Almost exactly four years before his own death, Harry suffered a severe loss when his son Whitfield died in a tragic accident.

Whitfield Wray Lipscomb was born on May 9, 1908. He spent much of his childhood in Lynchburg, where he lived with his sister, aunt, uncle and cousins. He began working as a teenager, as a store clerk and repairing shoes. He later moved back to Alexandria, where he lived with Harry at the Scottish Rite Club on North Alfred Street. (Harry was later noted as being a past master of the Scottish Rite Masons.)[96] Whitfield became an Alexandria police officer on August 2, 1929, at the age of twenty-one.

Just one year later, on the afternoon of September 4, 1930, Private Lipscomb was talking at the Potomac (present-day Del Ray), Virginia fire station when the alarm went off. There was a car and brush fire along Four Mile Road. Intending to direct traffic at the scene of the fire, Lipscomb jumped onto the back of the company's new fire engine, Engine No. 2, as the firefighters headed out.

As the fire engine sped north along what is today US Route 1, a truck cut in front of the crew just as they were nearing Four Mile Run. The firefighter at the wheel quickly swerved to try to avoid a collision. The large fire engine went into a ditch, overturning.

After being struck hard by the fire hose, Private Lipscomb was thrown from the engine, his neck broken and his skull fractured. Rushed to nearby Alexandria Hospital, the young police officer was pronounced dead at 2:30 p.m. Three firefighters injured in the accident recovered. The truck that had swerved in front of the firemen apparently kept going and was never identified.[97]

September 1934 saw Harry Acree Lipscomb boarding the *Morro Castle* along with another Southern Railway employee, Frederick George Faulconer. Originally from the small town of Barboursville, Virginia, Faulconer was the Southern Railway's chief dispatcher. He and Lipscomb had been provided passage via a pass from their company to the Ward Line, owners of the *Morro Castle*. Harry gave his address as 265 Commerce Street in Alexandria. He and Fred were accommodated in Cabin 227 on C Deck, just forward of the dining room.[98]

Whitfield rests next to his father. *Author's collection.*

According to *Morro Castle* researcher Jim Kalafus, for some unknown reason, the passenger cabins just forward of the dining room's upper level proved to be exceptionally lethal on the night of the fire. The majority of passengers whose bodies would never be found were accommodated in this area, and the cabins from this location that were reached by the blaze had 100 percent fatalities. Kalafus theorizes that these blocks of cabins were sealed off by the fire early on, forcing the occupants out of their portholes with no life preservers.[99]

Harry Lipscomb rests in Spring Hill Cemetery in Lynchburg. Note the misspelling of the family name. *Author's collection.*

In the case of Harry Acree Lipscomb and Fred Faulconer, their bodies were recovered. Faulconer was recovered and identified early in the search, while Lipscomb was not found for a number of days. Fred's body had washed ashore at Sea Girt, New Jersey. It was believed at the time that he had drowned while attempting to swim to shore. Frederick George Faulconer was later buried in Graham Cemetery in Orange, Virginia. Initially, there was speculation that Harry might have not boarded the *Morro Castle* at all. Unfortunately, this was not so.

This collage of previously unpublished images shows the burnt hulk of *Morro Castle* ashore at Asbury Park, New Jersey. *Author's collection.*

Late on the night of September 15, after having been in the ocean nearly one week, the body of Harry Acree Lipscomb washed ashore at Spring Lake, near Asbury Park, in New Jersey. Thanks to some paperwork found inside his pockets, a positive identification was made.[100] His granddaughter recalled hearing that her grandfather's body reportedly had no burns on it when found, lending credence to the theory that he might have jumped from his porthole before the fire reached the inside of his cabin. Ironically, Harry's death might have been hastened by his life jacket, the thick cork linings of which were known to knock jumpers unconscious on impact with the sea and possibly cause broken necks. Harry's body was transported from New Jersey to Alexandria the following day.

Harry's was one of three bodies of *Morro Castle* victims to be discovered on September 15. An unidentified male passenger, described as being about five feet, ten inches tall, a fifteen-jewel watch bearing no inscription in his pocket, was found at Manasquan, New Jersey. Meanwhile, at Point Pleasant, New Jersey, the body of a man clad in a sailor's jacket had come ashore in the early morning hours.[101]

According to Sandra, her grandfather was initially buried in a "Catholic cemetery" in Alexandria, where Whitfield had also been interred. But just

A second previously unpublished collage shows the area of Asbury Park, New Jersey, and the abandoned wreck of *Morro Castle. Author's collection.*

two months after losing her son on the *Morro Castle*, Harry's mother, Susan Pauline Lipscomb, passed away on November 5, 1934. She was buried in Spring Hill Cemetery. Afterward, Harry and Whitfield were exhumed from the Catholic cemetery and reinterred beside Susan in Lynchburg, both father and son being buried there on May 3, 1935.[102] The family name is misspelled on the headstones, including the errant "e."

Sandra Holt heard about her grandfather's death on the *Morro Castle* on rare occasions over the years, and never from her mother, who would "clam up" whenever Sandra asked about the grandfather she never knew. Sandra's mother was "a daddy's girl, and she loved him very, very much."[103]

Recovered from Harry and Fred's charred cabin on the *Morro Castle* were ten keys on a key ring, three keys on a key ring, two individual keys, one cufflink, one quarter, and one nickel.[104]

In addition to Whitfield, Sandra's mother lost her other brother, Harry Acree Lipscomb Jr., in a tragedy that occurred not long after their father's death at sea. On August 25, 1936, Harry Jr. was killed in a car accident while returning home with some friends after a day of target practice. He was twenty years old.[105]

It was a pleasant surprise to the granddaughter to learn that people are still interested in the *Morro Castle*, the tragedy that took away her grandfather, as well as other "smaller shipwrecks," and not just the *Titanic*.

7

PEARL HARBOR

U ntil September 11, 2001, any thought or mention of a sneak attack on the United States very likely conjured images of the quiet Sunday morning of December 7, 1941, when the naval base at Pearl Harbor was attacked by the Japanese. This "date which will live in infamy" proved to be the catalyst for our nation entering the Second World War, and the images of Japanese bombers zipping over our battleships and the USS *Arizona* ablaze in the harbor's waters are embedded in the minds of even the most novice of U.S. history students.

That Sunday morning in Hawaii had started out peacefully at Pearl Harbor. But by the afternoon, several brave young men from Southwest Virginia had made the ultimate sacrifice.

WILLIAM JAMES HOLZHAUER

William James Holzhauer was born on November 5, 1918, in Abingdon, Virginia. He was the fourth child born to John H. Holzhauer, a plumber, and his wife, Anna Black, a homemaker.[106] Entering the U.S. Navy just out of high school, Bill attained the rank of seaman first class, serving aboard the USS *Oklahoma* from 1937 until the morning of December 7, 1941. The *Oklahoma* was inflicted with several torpedo hits and capsized. A total of 429 of its crewmen lost their lives in the attack. One of them was Bill Holzhauer.

Two young men from Southwest Virginia lost their lives on the USS *Oklahoma* on December 7, 1941. *Wikimedia Commons.*

That afternoon, Abingdon barber Oscar B. Brown was listening to his favorite radio program when the broadcast was interrupted by an announcer stating that the Japanese had bombed Pearl Harbor. That evening, Brown recalled later, he and his family were about to have dinner. He had just finished asking the blessing when the radio announcer came back on with the latest casualty list. Brown ran to the radio and clearly heard a familiar name: "William Holzhauer, Abingdon, Virginia." With tears in his eyes, Brown recalled a little boy who "twisted in an oversized barber's chair as the tiny bits of hair fell down his face and down his neck." Brown had been William's barber "since he was just a baby."

On that day, Oscar Brown made a promise: he would never charge a nickel to cut any active serviceman's hair. And he stuck to it. It was, he felt, his way of fighting back against the Japanese bombers who took his young friend's life. What Brown did would not be forgotten.

On December 6, 1957, acting on a unanimous vote from their nine hundred members, the Abingdon VFW awarded the faithful barber a special "Service to Servicemen" award, consisting of an engraved plaque and a twenty-five-dollar savings bond. In a time of strict segregation and heavy

William J. Holzhauer's striking cenotaph stands in Sinking Spring Cemetery in Abingdon. *Author's collection.*

racial tensions, the award was perhaps doubly special for the Black barber. "I guess I'm about the happiest man alive," Brown said that day, tears streaming down his face.[107]

In historic Sinking Spring Cemetery in Abingdon, there is an impressive granite cenotaph for William Holzhauer. It features a carved impression of the USS *Oklahoma*. In 2018, previously unidentified remains from the National Memorial Cemetery of the Pacific in Honolulu, Hawaii, were positively identified as belonging to William James Holzhauer. At the time of this writing, what will ultimately become of the remains is yet to be stated.

WARREN HARDING CRIM

Warren Harding Crim was born on Thursday, October 13, 1921, in McMinnville, Warren County, Tennessee, to Vernon and Maude Maie Stubblefield Crim. Vernon was a farmer who also dug wells and cisterns and sometimes cut timber for the Mullion Lumber Company.

Warren attended McMinnville Grammar School, though during the years of the Depression his family frequently relocated, and he also attended schools in Bybee Branch, Lucky and other areas throughout the region. When he wasn't in school, young Warren helped his father on the farm and with his digging and timber-cutting. When Warren was a teenager, his parents divorced.

On April 5, 1939, Warren, along with his friend I.D. Byers, entered the Civilian Conservation Corps (CCC). For several months, Warren served with the CCC on Lookout Mountain before his unit was relocated to Bristol, Tennessee, in September 1939. It was in Bristol that Warren met Mildred Smith, the young lady who would become his wife. During their tour in Bristol, Warren and I.D. decided to volunteer for service in the navy. Warren enlisted on July 10, 1940, at age eighteen. In his physical examination, he was noted as standing five feet, eleven inches tall, with black hair, blue eyes and a ruddy complexion. Warren received his basic training at the Norfolk Naval Base in Norfolk, Virginia.

In the early months of Warren's career with the navy, he and Mildred were married. They lived at 104 East State Street in Bristol.

By December 7, 1941, Crim had attained the rank of fireman third class and was serving on the USS *Oklahoma*, along with Abingdon native William J. Holzhauer. *Oklahoma* received nine torpedo hits in the surprise attack. Along with 428 others on the vessel, Fireman Third Class Crim was killed that Sunday morning. Naval documents note that he, as many were known to have been, was likely trapped belowdecks in the attack. He was posthumously awarded the Purple Heart, the World War II Victory Medal and the American Defense Service Medal. Crim was Warren County's first casualty of World War II.[108]

Warren Harding Crim in a portrait taken during his brief time in the U.S. Navy. *Courtesy of Sam Crimm II.*

Personal effects of an unknown type were sent to Warren's widow, Mildred. This appears to have caused some consternation with Warren's mother, who had by this time remarried. The following letter from Rear Admiral William Furlong to Maude Craven, dated September 3, 1944, is preserved by Warren's family:

Dear Mrs. Craven:

Your letter dating 21 August 1944 regarding your son has been received.

Apparently my letter of 15 August crossed your letter in the mails but has no doubt been received by you now. Since the personal effects have already been shipped to your daughter-in-law, it is regrettable that there are no further effects to be sent you. However I am sending you a knife recovered from the USS Oklahoma *on which ship your son gave his life for his country.*

Unfortunately the next of kin is a legal matter and cannot now be changed.

Sincerely,
William R. Furlong
Rear Admiral, U.S. Navy[109]

Salvage operations were undertaken on the USS *Oklahoma* in 1943, at which time the recovery of those lost aboard it in the 1941 attack was begun. *Naval History and Heritage Command.*

The story of Warren Harding Crim does have a touching postscript. On January 19, 2018, remains disinterred from the National Memorial Cemetery of the Pacific (known as the Punchbowl) in Honolulu were positively identified as being those of Crim. The confirmation was made thanks to DNA testing, the research of which was spearheaded by Warren's second-oldest living cousin, Patricia Crim, of Morristown, Tennessee. On Saturday, October 24, 2020, Warren Harding Crim finally came home. That

Warren H. Crim's remains were interred in Gardens of Memory Cemetery in McMinnville, Tennessee, in 2020. *Courtesy of Sam Crimm II.*

afternoon, his earthly remains were interred in the Gardens of Memory Cemetery in McMinnville, Tennessee. Full military rights were performed by the U.S. Navy.[110]

HAYWOOD HUBBARD JR.

Haywood Hubbard Jr. was born on November 29, 1921, in Campbell County, Virginia, part of the Lynchburg metropolitan area. The biographical information presently available on Haywood is scant. His father, Haywood Sr., was working as a machine-cleaner at a paper mill, and his mother, Mary Scott Hubbard, was a homemaker. Another son, Henry, worked as an animal-skinner at a soap factory. During the destitute years of the Great Depression, the family reported that in 1939 they had earned a combined income of only $762 (roughly $14,000 in 2020) to support a family of seven.

Haywood Jr. enlisted in the U.S. Navy in August 1940 at the age of eighteen. Because he was Black, and the United States military was segregated at the time, there was only one option available to Haywood Jr.:

Haywood Hubbard Jr. was serving as a cook aboard USS *Arizona* on the morning of December 7, 1941. *National Archives and Records Administration.*

mess attendant.[111] In this capacity, he helped cook, cleaned the kitchen and mess hall and performed similar duties.

On December 7, 1941, Haywood Hubbard Jr. was serving as a mess attendant second class aboard the USS *Arizona*. On that fateful morning, when the 608-foot vessel was rocked by massive explosions, Haywood Jr. became one of the 1,771 souls lost on the ship. His body might still lie within the wreck, the broken steel hull his tomb and the waters of Pearl Harbor the cemetery.

8

USS *PERCH*

On April 11, 1942, as the United States' involvement in the Second World War was escalating, the navy announced the loss of the USS *Perch* (SS-176), one of its finest undersea craft. The submarine was, as of that date, overdue from a patrol in the Java Sea. The *Perch*, just over three hundred feet long and weighing over two thousand tons, was now feared to have been destroyed. This would make it the fifth U.S. submarine to have been lost during the war.

Newspapers reported that the commander of the USS *Perch* was a highly esteemed native of Pounding Mill, Virginia: thirty-eight-year-old Lieutenant Commander David Albert Hurt.

DAVID ALBERT HURT

Lieutenant Commander David Albert Hurt was born on August 4, 1903, in Tazewell County, Virginia, to John Bascomb and Olivia Louise Hurt. Young David attended Tazewell High School and, following graduation, he was a student at Hampton-Sydney College for a time. In 1921, Hurt received an appointment to the United States Naval Academy in Annapolis, Maryland, from Virginia senator Carter Glass.

Following his matriculation from the academy, Officer Hurt received his first assignment, aboard the USS *Raleigh*. He was then transferred to Submarine Division 12 in October 1928, reporting to the Naval Submarine

USS *Perch*, a *Porpoise*-class U.S. submarine, was scuttled in the Java Sea by its crew. *Naval History and Heritage Command.*

School in New London, Connecticut, in December. Hurt served aboard the submarine USS *R-14* (SS-91) until 1933, when he returned to the Naval Academy for postgraduate instruction.

After completion of his postgraduate work, Lieutenant Hurt served on the USS *S-34* (SS-139) until January 1935, whereupon he was placed in command of the USS *S-35* (SS-140) until May 1937, at which point he became an instructor in the U.S. Naval Academy's electrical engineering department until May 1939, when he was placed in command of the USS *Perch*.[112]

During this period, Lieutenant Commander Hurt and his family resided in Annapolis.[113] He and his first wife welcomed a son, David Albert Hurt Jr., on April 23, 1926.

On March 2, 1942, while carrying fifty-four enlisted men and five officers, the *Perch* was mortally damaged by depth charges in an attack carried out by the Japanese destroyers *Amatsukaze* and *Hatsukaze*. The U.S. submarine managed to dive, and its crew later made cursory repairs, in spite of the heavy damage incurred. Hours later, the *Perch* resurfaced, only to be quickly forced to dive again by the appearance of another enemy destroyer.

By the morning of March 3, despite having undergone the best repairs possible under the circumstances, the submarine was showing signs of heavy damage. After a near-disastrous test dive, *Perch* miraculously resurfaced. While further repair work was being attempted, three Japanese destroyers and two cruisers appeared close by and began firing on the American crew. The situation now being quite hopeless, Lieutenant Commander Hurt issued the final order: "Abandon ship. Scuttle the boat." With all hatches open, the *Perch* plummeted 190 feet down to the bottom of the Java Sea, where it would rest undetected in darkness until November 23, 2006, when a team of divers accidentally came across the wreck.[114] The

Lieutenant Commander David Albert Hurt was a native of Pounding Mill. *Naval History and Heritage Command.*

U.S. Navy officially struck the USS *Perch* from its Naval Vessel Register on June 24, 1942.

After the scuttling of their submarine, the fifty-nine American men were picked up by the Japanese destroyer *Ushio*. They were then disseminated to Japanese prisoner of war camps. Hurt was sent to Ōmori Camp in Tokyo, Japan. He was later recalled as having served as a "father figure"[115] to the younger officers he was enduring imprisonment with. In addition to being a father figure, Hurt was by now the father of three children back home.

Back in the United States, it was feared that the men of the *Perch* had lost their lives. In Hurt's case, this sentiment even reached the White House. President Franklin D. Roosevelt established a scholarship in Hurt's name at his alma mater, the U.S. Naval Academy.[116]

Six members of the USS *Perch*'s crew in fact died as prisoners of war. But Lieutenant Commander Hurt survived. Chief Electrician's Mate Houston Ernest Edwards died on July 10, 1944. Machinist's Mate Second Class Charles Newton Brown died of pellagra on April 18, 1945. Fire Controlman Robert A. Wilson of Weehawken, New Jersey, died of bacterial dysentery and pellagra on June 15, 1945. Pharmacist Philip James Dewes and Chief Machinist's Mate Albert Kenneth Newsome also died in captivity.[117]

The ultimate sacrifice made by Machinist's Mate First Class Frank Elmer McCreary is revered by his family to this day. Born on October 20, 1903, in St. Louis, Missouri, Frank enlisted in the U.S. Navy on August 4, 1922, at Little Rock, Arkansas, just before his nineteenth birthday. He served aboard

The *Perch*'s crew was taken prisoner by the Japanese destroyer *Ushio*. *Wikimedia Commons.*

the *Perch* during war patrols in 1941 and 1942 and was held captive as a POW in the Japanese Fukuoka Camp. Sadly, Frank passed away on January 4, 1943, after nearly one year of internment. His cause of death was given as acute pneumonia. His father, Daniel Edward McCreary, received the following letter, dated June 1, 1944, from the U.S. Navy Department, Bureau of Naval Personnel, Washington, D.C.:

> *On May 11, 1943 the Navy Department informed you that it was in receipt of an official cablegram from the International Red Cross in Tokyo, stating that your son, Frank Elmer McCreary, Machinist's Mate first class, U.S. Navy was being held as prisoner of war in Fukuoka Camp. It is now the duty of this Bureau to inform you that it is in receipt of an International Red Cross Committee Telegram dated 9 July 1943, stating that your son died in Fukuoka Camp as a result of acute pneumonia. From information given in the telegram it has been determined that the date of your son's death was 4 January 1943.[118]*

Shortly after the end of the war, Frank's former wife, Betty, wrote a letter to her former father-in-law asking for news of Frank. Remarried, Betty states that her second husband was also lost in a submarine during the war.

P.O. Box 793
San Francisco, California
January 19, 1946

Dear dad,

I know you will be surprised to hear from me after all these years. I didn't have your address but found Frank's cousin Sister Callista, and wrote to her to find out where you were. Frank and I were divorced in 1937, and the last time I seen him was in 1938. I remarried again and I lost my husband two years ago on a submarine. I heard that Frank was lost on the Perch at the start of the war. Have you heard anything lately? I am making my home here in San Francisco now and like it fine. Has Frank an aunt that lives here somewhere in San Francisco? I am sorry to hear of Frank's Aunt Cora passing away. Would like very much to hear from you soon.

Sincerely,
Betty
Mrs. V.R. Drake
P.O. Box 793
San Francisco, California[119]

After suffering through the living hell of a POW camp for over two years, Lieutenant Commander David Albert Hurt and the fifty-two other survivors from the *Perch*'s crew were liberated at the end of the war. For his outstanding service during the war, Hurt was awarded a Purple Heart, Navy Commendation Medal, Submarine Combat Pin with two stars, Prisoner of War Medal, American Defense Service Medal and Asiatic Pacific Campaign Medal.

The lieutenant commander arrived home to Annapolis, Maryland, undoubtedly a very thankful man, in August 1945. Southwest Virginia remained close to his heart, and within a few months, he took a trip back to his original home, where tragedy would unexpectedly strike this newly freed war hero.

At approximately 11:00 a.m. on November 21, 1945, the day before his first Thanksgiving back home,[120] David Hurt was hunting quails on the Elk Garden, Virginia property of H.O. Pratt along with two friends, Dr. Brittain and Dr. John McGuire, of Bluefield. (Dr. McGuire was also related to Hurt.) The doctors had gone over a hillside ahead of the commander

Left: Frank Elmer McCreary served as machinist's mate first class on the *Perch*'s final patrol. *Courtesy of Marian Brune McCreary.*

Below: Commander Hurt's humble grave marker is in Jeffersonville Cemetery in Tazewell. *Author's collection.*

when they suddenly heard a muffled gunshot. Returning over the hill, they found Lieutenant Commander Hurt lying lifeless on the ground, mortally wounded in the head.[121] It appeared he had tripped over a tangle of vines that were prevalent in the immediate area where his body was found, his gun falling and discharging the fatal shot.[122] He was forty-two years old.

After having survived World War II, the scuttling of the USS *Perch* and the horrors of a Japanese POW camp, the commander died instantly following an accident with his own gun. It was a sudden and tragic end to an exemplary life.

David Albert Hurt, a true American hero whose name should be on the lips of all locals, rests in the old Jeffersonville Cemetery in Tazewell, his humble granite marker overtaken by lichen moss and unkempt grass.

9

DOUGHBOYS AND GIs

The term *doughboy* was used to refer to the young soldiers of World War I. The exact origins of the term remain mysterious, though this nickname for these brave young men has persisted to this day. *GI* (general infantry) is a rather generic term that came to prominence years later, during World War II, and is still common military vernacular today. Of course, the most famous example is the action figure and comic hero GI Joe. The following stories provide only a sliver of the experiences of the many thousands of young men from Southwest Virginia who served—and often gave their lives for—their country during these two monumental conflicts.

USS *CYCLOPS*

For some readers, the death of William Bryan Brooks of Roanoke, Virginia, might have a tinge of the supernatural about it. Brooks, about which extremely little biographical information could be found, served as a seaman aboard the USS *Cyclops*.[123] The 542-foot vessel departed Brazil in February 1918 bound for Baltimore, Maryland, with a heavy load of manganese ore, a load that was later believed to have exceeded the vessel's capacity. The crew had also reported trouble with the *Cyclops*'s engines. Though the reason would never be conclusively explained, the USS *Cyclops* failed to make port in Baltimore on March 13, its scheduled arrival date. No trace of the ship or its crew were ever found. On June 1, 1918, the ship was officially declared lost and all its hands, including William Bryan Brooks, dead.[124]

The ultimate fate of the USS *Cyclops* remains a mystery. *Wikimedia Commons.*

Over the century-plus since its disappearance, many theories have been put forth in an attempt to explain what happened to the *Cyclops*. Many of these explanations are outlandish, involving UFO abduction and, most famously, the Bermuda Triangle. The most likely cause of the ship's disappearance is that it met with bad weather and, overloaded with manganese ore and already experiencing engine problems, went down in heavy seas.

RMS *SAMARIA*

Before the United States joined World War II, a number of refugees from the warring nations were making their way to our shores. On August 28, 1940, the Cunard Line's RMS *Samaria* arrived in New York carrying 183 children from England who were coming to the United States. Among them were eight-year-old Shirley Ann Sheehan and her five-year-old brother, Anthony Quentin. The children were to make their home with Mr. and Mrs. James W. McClung in Lexington, Virginia, until the cessation of war in their home country. The children were originally from London, England.[125]

USS *ENTERPRISE*

The historic Battle of Midway was waged in the Pacific from June 4 to 7, 1942, during the height of World War II. Marking a pivotal victory for the United States, the battle was the basis for an eponymous blockbuster film in 2019. Few in Southwest Virginia likely know that among the Americans who fought valiantly over that fateful four days was a young man originally from Grundy.

His name was Arthur James Davis. Born about 1920 in Grundy, his death has been erroneously listed as having occurred at the Battle of Midway. It did not, though Arthur did ultimately give his brief life for his country. Spending his early years in Grundy, Arthur's family later relocated to Bluefield, Virginia. Around 1935, the Davises again moved, this time to Brush Fork, West Virginia, where Arthur attended Beaver High School.

The youth enlisted in the navy on December 12, 1937, probably just a few months shy of his eighteenth birthday. A boatswain's mate first class, Davis served aboard the legendary USS *Enterprise*. On December 7, 1941, the *Enterprise* was the only carrier to successfully get U.S. planes into action during the Japanese attack on Pearl Harbor.

After surviving both Pearl Harbor and the Battle of Midway, the USS *Enterprise* and PO Davis were again engaged against the Japanese in the Battle of the Eastern Solomons, which began on August 24, 1942, and lasted through the following day. On August 24, this local hero made the ultimate sacrifice, giving his life for his country at age twenty-two. Davis was struck by gunfire while running across the *Enterprise*'s deck to put out a fire. Arthur Davis was one of ninety U.S. casualties that occurred in the battle.

Lieutenant S.B. Strong, another member of the *Enterprise*'s crew, later wrote to Arthur's parents: "At the time, the ship was engaged in a desperate struggle with a ruthless and determined foe. Though the full circumstance concerning the action must be withheld in the interest of security, I can say it was by the skill, courage and devotion to duty such as shown by your son that we were successful."[126]

Boatswain's Mate First Class Davis was posthumously awarded the Purple Heart. But a bigger honor lay ahead. On December 30, 1944, in Charleston, South Carolina, the U.S. Navy launched the USS *Chimariko* in honor of Arthur James Davis. The new fleet tug was christened by the young man's mother, who, in addition to his father and several other members of the family, were present at the launching. The new vessel did not bear the seaman's name, as the navy already had a vessel in use called the USS *Arthur Davis*.

TYPHOON COBRA

The Typhoon Cobra, sometimes referred to as Halsey's Typhoon or the Typhoon of 1944, was a horrific cyclone that struck in the Philippine Sea in December 1944, overtaking Task Force 38 of the United States Pacific Fleet. Three destroyers were sunk in the maelstrom, resulting in the loss of 790 American lives. Among the lost were at least 2 young sailors from Southwest Virginia.

John Alexander Litton of Rocky Station, Virginia, was one of eleven children of James Duff and Nancy Jane Rasnick Litton. Leaving Pennington High School during his senior year in order to enlist in the navy, Litton had been a member of the crew aboard the USS *Monaghan* since 1941. Two of his brothers also served in the navy. Beginning with the December 7, 1941 attack on Pearl Harbor, Litton was said to have been in sixteen major engagements, and he had been awarded the Good Conduct Medal.[127]

By December 1944, Litton held the rank of yeoman third class. On December 18, Task Force 38, a group of American destroyers, battleships, carriers and cruisers that had been raiding Japanese airfields in the

John Litton of Pennington Gap lost his life on the USS *Monaghan*. *Naval History and Heritage Command.*

WHITE WILLIAM R	· ·	AVN RADIOMAN 2C	· ·	USN	· ·	KANSAS
WHITED CLEO P	· ·	SEAMAN IC	· ·	USNR	· ·	VIRGINIA
WHITEFORD JACK E	· ·	SIGNALMAN 3C	· ·	USN	· ·	CALIFORNIA

Top: Cleo P. Whited of Swords Creek went down with the USS *Spence* during the Typhoon Cobra. *Wikimedia Commons.*

Bottom: Cleo Parson Whited is memorialized on the Walls of the Missing in the Manila American Cemetery in the Philippines. *Author's collection.*

Philippines, was in the process of being refueled when it was struck by the typhoon. The USS *Monaghan*, along with the *Spence* and *Hull*, capsized.

Yeoman Third Class Litton was one of 256 crewmen on the *Monaghan* to lose his life that day. Only a scant 6 members of its crew survived. These fortunate few were recovered by the USS *Brown*, exhausted and in shock after being exposed to the relentless sea for four days. John Alexander Litton's body was never recovered.

Another of the 790 lives lost that terrible day was Cleo Parson Whited of Swords Creek, Virginia. Born on April 19, 1923, Cleo was the son of William David and Ida Ellen Whited.[128] According to a nephew, Cleo was sometimes called Parley, though the reason for the nickname has been forgotten.

Seaman Whited was serving aboard the USS *Spence*, another one of the three destroyers lost on December 18, 1944. Cleo was one of 317 crewmen of that vessel who lost their lives at the hands of the unrelenting typhoon. There were only 23 survivors from the *Spence*. As with Litton, the body of Seaman Whited was never recovered. A cenotaph was placed in his memory in the small family cemetery in Swords Creek.

USS BUNKER HILL

The following biography was written by Katy Jo Arrington Powers, a former science teacher at Haysi High School, in memory of her brother Daniel Ray Arrington. Dan lost his life on May 11, 1945, while serving his country aboard the USS *Bunker Hill* when the aircraft carrier was attacked by Japanese kamikaze fighter planes. Mrs. Powers passed away while this book was being written. I can think of no better way to preserve the memories of both Mrs. Powers and her heroic brother, whom she obviously loved very much, than to present her words as she wrote them.

Daniel Ray Arrington, better known as Dan, was the only son of William H. and Alta Fuller Arrington. Dan was born at Haysi, Virginia on December 26, 1919. He had one sister, Katy Jo Arrington Powers. He resided in Haysi most of his short life. He was educated at Haysi Elementary and Haysi High School and also attended Berea College and Bluefield Business College.

He married Julia O. Cooper and was the father of two daughters, Katherine Sue and Martha Jean.

Up until the time he went into the navy he was the manager of Breaks Motor Corporation, the Ford Dealership at Haysi, Virginia.

He chose the navy as the branch of service he wanted in order to get in; he entered the navy at Camp Perry, Virginia on April 28, 1944 and was sent to Perdue University at Lafayette, Indiana for communications specialist training. After graduation he was sent to Shoemaker, California for training and was assigned to the famous flat-top aircraft carrier, the USS Bunker Hill, *one of the largest aircraft carriers of the Pacific. Its planes provided air support for the invasion of Iwo Jima, Okinawa and several other islands. The ship took part in the attacks on Tokyo, Japan, February 16, 17, and 25, 1945. The ship was known as Admiral Mitchel's Flat Ship 58 Task Force and was in active duty for fifty-eight days before being hit by a Japanese suicide plane on May 11, 1945. Dan was killed off the coast of Okinawa when the kamikaze pilot struck the large flat-top damaging it greatly. He was buried at sea the following day on May 12, 1945, along with other shipmates who were killed there. He received posthumously the Purple Heart and several other medals. He has a military marker in Russell Memorial Cemetery, Lebanon, Virginia, near his parents. His name is also inscribed in a memorial at Honolulu, Hawaii as well as the Clintwood Courthouse.*[129]

USS *Bunker Hill* was struck by Japanese kamikaze fighter planes. *Naval History and Heritage Command.*

Daniel Ray Arrington was buried at sea. He is memorialized by this cenotaph in Russell Memorial Cemetery in Lebanon. *Edgar A. Rice Collection.*

Katy Jo was not the only local to revere the memory of Daniel Ray Arrington. Edgar A. Rice made Dan the center of a personal Memorial Day tradition: "Every Memorial Day I visit Daniel Ray Arrington's military marker in Lebanon, Virginia and place a plaque with two American flags and his picture. As I visited Haysi High School in May 2015 for the final time before the closing of the grand old school, there was a picture of Daniel wearing his navy uniform hanging in the hallway down from the principal's office. Haysi High School was honoring one of its own who gave his life in the defense of his country."

RMS QUEEN MARY

For Stuart Richardson of Russell County, Virginia, his first sight of the Cunard Line's monstrous RMS *Queen Mary* must have been unforgettable. The transatlantic liner, over one thousand feet in length, was to provide his transportation home following his service in World War II. Its hull, superstructure and funnels were painted in a hazy gray camouflage, earning the *Queen Mary* the wartime nickname "The Gray Ghost."

His quarters being located deep within the bowels of the ship, Stuart found his journey home boring. At some point, he began amusing himself

The *Queen Mary* transported many thousands of U.S. soldiers both to and from the battlefields of World War II. *Author's collection.*

with a ceramic Cunard Line cup, at which he would toss loose coins to see if he could get them into the cup. In this way he invented a little game to amuse himself. Stuart then decided to test the strength of the ceramic cup by dropping it from his bunk onto an iron L beam to see if it would chip or crack. According to Stuart's son Harold, the cup never received a chip or a crack! Stuart was so impressed by the cup's durability that he decided to keep it, and it is still in the possession of someone in his family.[130]

10

VARIOUS STORIES

This final chapter presents a series of stories and snippets of information that would not fit in any of the other chapters of this book. Some of the historical links presented here are quite tangential, but they will still be of note to those with an interest in maritime history. Others offer direct links to major events, and they might be surprising to learn about. As with the other stories in this book, the events detailed in this chapter are presented in chronological order.

RMS *TEUTONIC*

In September 1890, it was reported in the local news that documents relating to a $1 million deal involving the services of the Big Stone Gap Improvement Company were being transported to England via the RMS *Teutonic*, a now-classic steamship owned by the White Star Line. The story stated that the gentleman in charge of the papers had "reasonable hopes of a speedy and favorable outcome." The ultimate outcome could not be determined.[131]

RMS *ARABIC*

In the fall of 1903, Mrs. Blanche B. Silliman, a socialite from Salem, Virginia, undertook a sea voyage to Europe with her husband aboard the

RMS *Teutonic*, here seen at the landing stage in Liverpool, carried an important proposal from Big Stone Gap. *Author's collection.*

RMS *Arabic*, a then-new steamship owned by the White Star Line. Blanche kept a detailed diary of the entire crossing, which she then sent to the editors of the *Salem Times-Register*, where it was printed in full. On August 19, 1915, the *Arabic* met an untimely end at the hands of a U-boat during World War I.

The following are Blanche's published diary entries in their entirety. Only very minor grammatical changes have been made by me to ensure clarity for the reader. The modern reader should be mindful of the fact that Blanche was writing at a time far removed from ours, and that certain discussions mentioned in her diary entries would today be considered offensive.

October 2nd, 1903.

Our state-room is No. 20, on the Promenade Deck just between the Saloon (dining) and upper Promenade or Boat Deck. It is just across from the baths, and is quite large and commodious having an extension bed, a lounge, which can be turned into a bed, a wardrobe, and other necessary belongings to a well-appointed state-room.

There are about a hundred first class passengers. The service is fine; the furnishings beautiful, and all that could be desired.

Many friends came down to see us off—dear Virginia friends, who have lived in New York some 20 or more years, came down to see us to extend congratulations and wish us a "bon voyage." At 2 all visitors were notified to leave, and wet eyes and wet handkerchiefs were plentiful. As the boat drew out, the white handkerchiefs fluttered, and the last farewells looked, and words of cheer and good wishes wafted out upon the air. We watched the receding sky-scrapers of New York and shore for quite a while—who shall say with what thoughts. But it soon thought us that there was a last chance to send a word to loved ones, so we hastened to the library to write a few lines to them and send by the pilot when he left us at Sandy Hook, so we wrote busily for an hour or so. At four the pilot had guided us safely out of the "Narrows" and left us to guide in later some other vessel to the shore. The afternoon was pleasant, but we were tired and took a good nap before dinner at 7. We were quite hungry then—and such a good dinner— to which we did ample justice, from "blue points" to nuts and fruits and figs. Our seats are 156–158 at the Purser's table. After dinner we went on upper deck and sat and drank in the delicious air. By and by, when the dinner had somewhat digested, we promenaded until we were ready to retire, at about 10 p.m. We were soon snug in bed, with every comfort—at perfect ease and happy that we were living to enjoy such a voyage that had thus begun so auspiciously.

October 3.—A most restful night—not a qualm yet! After a delightful salt bath, we were ready for breakfast. My bill of fare was "cantaloupe, oat meal, steak, eggs, rolls, coffee." The day is fine—clear, sunshiny, a bit cooler—but not cold yet. Everyone seems to be having a good time, which that there are no one sea sick, at least none on deck. I was talking to a lady at breakfast—at 8:30. We are now on deck in our chairs, under our rugs, enjoying the fine salt air. Our mileage today up to 12 is 270 miles.—These are such large, heavy boats, the motion is quite quiet, and the tables and beds never have to be protected with sideboards, so while they are slower by two or three days than the fast Lucania, Teutonic, etc., and those of the North German line, they are preferable from the standpoint of room and comfort in every respect. We shall always try to get on the big White Star liners.

As yet the passengers have not broken the ice of reserve, but are taken up with their individual plans. The lunch was quite enjoyed. In the afternoon we took a long nap. The salt air and exercise on deck made us enjoy a three-hour one before we realized it.

Our state-room is heated—just press a little button, or turn one, and you can have or get almost anything you wish. The steward or stewardess is at your beck and call—just have to raise your finger and press against the bell.

Dinner was fine.

October 4—Sunday—Salt bath at 8. What boons these are—so stimulating to the system. We had another fine, restful night. There has been no attack from the enemy—sea sickness. True, we have been taking Brush's Preventive, but the sea has been so smooth, and this giant steamer such a controlling element, that so far it has been smooth.

A good breakfast.

At 10:30 we had the Episcopal service, and most everyone attended.— Collection was taken for the maimed sailors, to be equally divided between those in New York and Liverpool—$34 was raised. At 11:30 bouillon was passed around on deck, and it felt very grateful to the stomach. Lunch at 1:30. We have gone 355 miles today.

At our end of the table we have some very interesting talkers. Next to Mr. Silliman is a young lace merchant who buys his goods in Nottingham and Berlin. I am at the end of one side. At the foot sits a man whose position in life we haven't been able to place—he might be most anything, but he knows the world. He has traveled on every sea and in every land on the globe, and he talks and entertains you. Just opposite is an Englishman with his wife and daughter. This is his thirty fourth trip across. You always count both ways—it sounds just twice as much, you know.

It has been cooler today, and we have put on our heavy underwear.—Just before lunch we got into conversation with an Englishman whose steamer chair is next to mine. Our chairs are all numbered and placed in a certain spot upon deck, and the steward places them there daily for us, and also cares for our rugs. This Englishman was returning from a trip—his first one—to this country.—He had visited Albany, New York, Boston, and many of the larger cities on the Atlantic coast, making his chief stop in New Orleans. He was charmed with our country. He says the English are just now intensely interested in our negro question. He has been looking into the situation, and is now writing quite an article about the question for a leading London paper. He read us what he had written, and we both gave him many points. It was very interesting to hear the subject discussed from an Englishman's standpoint, and it was absolutely delightful to give to an intelligent man some true data of the situation. We saw several ships; one passed—a quicker steamer.

October 5—Monday—The morning begun bright, cold and sunshiny, but became intermittently one cast with clouds. Felt a little sickish upon arising, but the salt bath, a dose of Brush's Preventive and an appetizing breakfast cured me. Our vis-à-vis at the table are warming up, and we have quite pleasant conversations three times a day. The one at the foot we found out is one of a firm in Newark, N.J., of gramophones, etc., also automobiles and pianolas. He has been introducing these all over the world; hence his travel.

It is much rougher today, and while we have not been at all sick, yet we have been quiet and taken many rests. Our Englishman—the solicitor from London—has been ill all day. Enjoyed lunch, a long siesta, a walk and sitting out on deck, dinner, and now am snug in bed, writing. It is quite cold. We are off the banks of Newfoundland and have come 364 miles today.

Tuesday—Notwithstanding the rather rough weather, we had a good night. It was somewhat of a struggle to get up as we were tossing. But after the finest salt bath, our courage rose, and after breakfast we felt positively frisky. The air is cold and invigorating—the sky overcast with clouds. We see gulls, and a vessel now and then. Our friends across at the table are the Pillings from Philadelphia. They are great travelers. The pater familias is a Yorkshire man. This is the fourth day out, and we haven't been ill—so very grateful, and I consider it remarkable for me. Am faithfully studying the "Baedeker" so that I will know what I want to see. Have seen three whales today, spouting water high in the air. We have traveled 345 miles. The Lucania *passed us, having left a day after, and will arrive a day earlier.*

Mrs. C.H. Silliman kept a detailed diary of her voyage aboard the *Arabic. Author's collection.*

We are enjoying everything very much not sick at all. Had a fine dinner. Most of the ladies dress for the evening meal, and many of the gentlemen put on their dress suits. Our Yorkshire man who lives in Philadelphia is a manufacturer of all cotton goods. The young lady is quite handsome, and is growing more and more popular. The couple next them lived in South Africa for 20 years, belong to the great middle class. Our London solicitor is writing an article on Texas. My husband is giving him data, so I feel that she will not suffer in his hands. We retired at 10:30.

BLANCHE B. SILLIMAN.[132]

SS *MERION*

In October 1904, it was reported that 840 head of cattle, each averaging approximately 1,500 pounds, were being shipped in two solid trainloads from Glade Spring, Virginia, to Philadelphia, Pennsylvania. Livestock experts were reported as having appraised the cattle as being "the finest ever shipped from Southwest Virginia." The shippers were J.S. Gillespie of Tazewell County, George W. Moss of Burkes Garden and the Huff brothers of Glade Spring.

Upon the arrival of the trains in Philadelphia twenty-eight hours later, on October 13, the cattle were herded aboard the American Line steamer SS *Merion*, bound for Liverpool. It was noted in the news that the gentlemen expected to make "a similar shipment" on October 22.[133]

RMS *CEDRIC*

February 1907 saw Judge John D. Horsley leaving his home in Bedford, Virginia, for New York City, where he boarded the RMS *Cedric*, one of the White Star Line's fabled "Big Four," to undertake a journey to Gibraltar, Naples and other points of interest in the Mediterranean. His journey was made not simply for leisure; rather, the judge had booked his crossing at the behest of his physicians, who believed that his health would benefit by the voyage. The health problems ailing the judge were not disclosed, but it was noted that he was expected to be gone for a month or longer.[134]

RMS *MAURETANIA*

Quite a large mishap occurred when Colonel Henry C. Stuart of Elk Garden, Virginia, future governor of Virginia, and his family arrived at Pier 54 from Europe aboard the Cunard Line's legendary RMS *Mauretania* on May 27, 1910. A misunderstanding originated when the colonel declared Mrs. Stuart, originally of Rich Valley, in Smyth County, Virginia, his daughter and her governess to be nonresidents when filling out the family's declaration forms. Colonel Stuart did this because of the fact that his family had been living abroad since 1908. Until very recently, this would have been the correct thing to do. However, unbeknownst to the Stuarts, a recent amendment to Section 709 of the Tariff Act of

Virginia governor Henry Carter Stuart is shown here later in life. *Wikimedia Commons.*

1909 stated that American citizens who had lived abroad for more than two years could no longer claim exemption as nonresidents, unlike only weeks earlier, when they were expected to do so. According to the colonel, the American consulate in Paris had given the couple "no hint" of this change in regulations.

As a result of the misunderstanding, the port authorities seized eight of Mrs. Stuart's steamer trunks, of a total of twenty-five pieces of baggage, and sent them to the public stores as containing valuable goods that were not declared.

> *There were several painful moments on the dock while the inspector uncovered a large array of new gowns, a dozen and more, many pairs of silken hose, some very handsome jewels—the inspector thought that one necklace would essay at about $3,000—and other articles of apparel and adornment. Mrs. Stuart had declared six gowns as dutiable, and on these her husband paid $300 duty on the dock because Mrs. Stuart wanted to use them immediately, and she did not relish the prospect of having all of her clothes sent to the public stores building.*[135]

Though port authorities never seemed to consider that the Stuarts had intended any wrongdoing in filling out their declaration forms, the incident did attract a good deal of embarrassing attention from the press. Colonel

Stuart, who was then a congressional candidate in the Ninth District of Virginia, sent the following lengthy statement to the *Richmond Evening Journal*:

New York, May 27.

As is well known in Virginia, my family has been abroad for considerably more than two years, having been detained there for the last sixteen months by illness. Under the latest circulars issued or recognized by the various consuls abroad, it has been published authoritatively, as representing the Treasury Department of the United States, that all persons who have been abroad continuously for two years may elect to enter American ports as non-residents, duty free, without thereby affecting citizenship. Acting on this ruling, which I, together with all others with whom I met, relied upon, I made out my own personal declaration as a resident of America, and made out the declaration of my wife, daughter and governess as non-residents.

On arrival in New York I was informed by one of the revenue officers that a new ruling had been made, under which no member of a family, even though they had been abroad two years, could enter free unless the head of the house had also been abroad two years. It was then too late to change the original declaration of my family, and the only question then was the value of the articles purchased abroad. Mrs. Stuart stated that her purchases abroad amounted to about $1,000, not counting a sealskin coat, specifically referred to in a letter from the consul general at Paris to the collectors or inspectors of the port of New York, and not counting a piece of ermine which she had carried abroad with her, but which had been put in new form. She was naturally unprepared and unable on the spur of the moment to make an itemized statement of purchases extending over two years, and stated that the articles could be examined and appraised, which was subsequently done.

It is to be regretted that the newspapers should have failed to present the exact facts in the case as to show that there was no intention on my part or the part of any member of my family to violate the law in the matter of declaration or otherwise. Concerning the jewels which were said to have been brought in, I wish to say that nothing of the kind was brought in by Mrs. Stuart during her absence. She had only the few modest ornaments which she took away with her, the most of which she has had for a number of years. She carried abroad seven trunks and brought back eight.

I followed strictly the latest published rulings obtainable, including that which was referred to as an authority by the printed declaration itself, and I indignantly repel the intimation of any purpose to violate the law in

The Stuarts were detained following their arrival aboard RMS *Mauretania* in 1910. *Author's collection.*

any way whatsoever. One of the higher revenue officials stated to and in the presence of several associates and subordinates that he was obliged to admit that the published literature of the department had not been kept abreast with the rulings. One of the inspectors stated that he himself was in ignorance of the ruling in question till it was announced in my case.

I wish to further add that a number of the observations alleged to have been made on the dock by members of my family were gross misrepresentations of facts.[136]

RMS *OLYMPIC*

The Woman's Christian Temperance Union (WCTU) was a national religious organization devoted to outlawing the sale and use of alcohol, many years before the advent of Prohibition. A notice published in Southwest Virginia newspapers in June 1911 regarding the Salem Union of the WCTU stated that a gentleman who had recently taken a transatlantic crossing "on one of the great White Star liners" had asked a steward of the ship whether, from what he had observed, liquor-drinking was increasing or decreasing among travelers. The steward was said to have replied that the sale of liquors was then "not more than one-quarter" what it was ten years before. "That is certainly a bit of spray to show which way the ship goes," opined the writer of the piece.[137]

The great White Star liner taken by the gentleman mentioned in the preceding story might have been the RMS *Olympic*, which completed its maiden voyage as the largest steamship in the world on June 21, 1911. The newspapers in Bedford, Virginia, had an interesting comparison regarding the monstrous new leviathan. "This means that every inhabitant of Bedford City could be loaded on this ship and travel with plenty of room and in comfort."[138]

INTERNATIONAL MERCANTILE MARINE

In June 1912, just two months after the momentous loss of its *Titanic*, a representative of the International Mercantile Marine (IMM), Edward J. Schembri, came to Bristol. The purpose of his visit was to assess Southwest Virginia's famous coal-mining operations, with the possible result being a partnership with IMM to supply its steamships with Southwest Virginian coal. IMM was the massive shipping conglomerate owned by J.P. Morgan. It controlled the White Star Line, American Line and Leyland Line, as well as others. The United Kingdom had suffered from several large mining strikes in recent months, and this might have been the impetus for the representative's visit. A deal with IMM to supply its vessels with coal would have been an amazing economic opportunity for our region, but sadly, it appears to have never gotten beyond initial assessments and discussions.

The representative's interests were centered on the operations along three railways: the Carolina, Clinchfield and Ohio; the Virginia and Southwestern; and the Norfolk and Western. Schembri was said to have had much experience in mining districts, having traversed the globe fourteen times. In Bristol, he stated:

> *If this section wants to come to the front in mining, like Northern and Western Pennsylvania, West Virginia and at present Alabama, it must welcome the foreign laborer. There should be no prejudice or antagonism toward him because he is essential to the development of the vast natural resources of this section. The Hungarians, Slavs, Poles and Italians are sober, peaceable people. The Syrians and Greeks are fine merchants and all of these as a rule make good citizens. It is important to keep out others who prey upon these plain, honest people.[139]*

SS *LAFAYETTE*

On June 23, 1916, the *Clinch Valley News* ran a notice that was attention-grabbing and, as it turned out, hilarious. It was reported that in the middle of the ocean, the steamer *Lafayette* had come across a bottle containing a note. The retrieved note was said to have read as follows:

To my friends in Tazewell, Va.—

When you find this bottle containing this note I will be no more. The boat Saratoga, *on which I am, has struck a leak and is fast sinking. In a few minutes it will be resting on the bottom of this roaring ocean. I take this method of sending my farewell words to my friends, trusting that some steamer may locate this bottle. And now I am sinking, and as I sink it is with one great regret—*that I will be unable to attend the Red Tag Sale at Chapman's on July 5th. Such Wonderful Bargains!**[140]

RMS *OLYMPIC*

Nancy Witcher Langhorne Astor, Viscountess Astor, was a native of Danville, Virginia. Residing in England, Lady Astor arrived in New York aboard the *Olympic* in April 1922. On April 15, it was announced that Danville had named "Astor Avenue" in her honor and that a telegram containing the announcement and an invitation for Lady Astor to visit Danville for a celebration during her stay had been dispatched to New York to await the arrival of *Olympic*.[141]

Nancy Witcher Langhorne Astor, Viscountess Astor, was originally from Danville. *Wikimedia Commons.*

CUNARD LINE

In 1924, Joe Soluri, a grocer in Norton, Virginia, sometimes referred to as the "Watermelon King," became an agent with the Cunard Line, whereby he could sell first- and second-class passenger tickets for the line's steamships at his grocery store.[142] His advertisements appeared frequently in area newspapers.

Norton grocer Joe Soluri became a Cunard Line agent in 1924. *Author's collection.*

RMS *CANOPIC*

It was announced on August 8, 1921, that the Reverend Dr. J.W. Smith and Mrs. Smith of Roanoke, Virginia, had left their home the night before, headed to New York. There, the couple boarded the White Star Line's RMS *Canopic* for Naples. The Smiths would visit Italy, Switzerland and the recently vacated World War I battlefields of France before attending the Methodist Ecumenical Conference in London from September 6 to 16. Afterward, the couple planned to spend a few days in Scotland, returning home by way of Canada, with the intention of arriving home around the first week of October.

Reverend Dr. Smith was the pastor of Greene Memorial Church, the congregation of which had voted him a leave of absence of seven weeks. Some of the church members had presented the Smiths with a purse of sufficient funds to pay the expenses of their extensive journey.[143]

SS *UNITED STATES*

When the SS *United States* departed for its maiden voyage on, appropriately, July 4, 1952, it was poised to take back dominance of the seas for America. The ship was hailed as a wonder, and it still has many devotees to this day, so it is little wonder that it was used in various advertisements, as were many ocean liners before it. Appalachian Electric Power Company used the ship in an ad that ran in newspapers throughout the region in an attempt to get residents to turn to electric cooking.[144]

Appalachian Electric Power Company featured SS *United States* in a 1952 advertisement. *Wikimedia Commons.*

SS ANDREA DORIA

For most people with a casual interest in maritime history, the SS *Andrea Doria*, which sank on July 25, 1956, is likely the most recent of the famous shipwrecks they can name off the top of their head. For several residents of Lexington, Virginia, news of the sinking hit them as though "they had lost a good friend."[145] Dr. and Mrs. L.J. Desha and Dr. and Mrs. William Jenks had gone abroad aboard the Italian passenger steamer on June 8, 1954, for a three-month visit to Europe.[146]

Robert L. Moore, U.S. Coast Guard, of Buena Vista, Virginia, had a front-row view of the sinking. Assigned to the U.S. Coast Guard cutter *Hornbeam*, Moore wrote home to his parents in early August 1956, advising them that his vessel had participated in the rescue of the passengers from the *Andrea Doria* on July 25. "It was a sad experience," he wrote to his parents, Mr. and Mrs. Henry Moore.[147] Regrettably, a copy of his entire letter appears not to have been provided to the newspaper.

For young Phillip Bechman of Naperville, Illinois, who was visiting his grandmother on Park Street in Bedford, Virginia, at around the time of the *Doria*'s sinking, the timing of a gift had a peculiarity to it. Phillip's aunt, Mrs. A.P. Montague of Lynchburg, Virginia, brought the boy a toy model of the *Andrea Doria* when she returned from the beach, just a few days before the actual ship collided with the Norwegian collier *Storstad* and sank.[148]

Taken from an airplane, this aerial view shows the sinking *Andrea Doria* listing heavily to starboard. A lifeboat full of survivors is rescued in the foreground. *Wikimedia Commons.*

Robert L. Moore of Buena Vista helped rescue survivors of the *Andrea Doria* while serving on the U.S. Coast Guard cutter *Hornbeam*. *Naval History and Heritage Command.*

American Red Cross advertisements, run in Southwest Virginia newspapers in early 1957, featured an unnamed little boy receiving a new pair of shoes from the Red Cross. He was described as being one of the survivors of the *Andrea Doria*, though his name was not recorded.[149]

NOTES

1. SS *Columbia*

1. Historical Data Systems Inc.; Duxbury, MA 02331; American Civil War Research Database.
2. *Journal and Tribune* (Knoxville, TN), July 25, 1907.
3. *Journal and Tribune*, January 30, 1907.
4. *Tazewell (VA) Republican*, July 25, 1907.
5. *The Insurance Times*, October 1907.
6. *Journal and Tribune*, July 27, 1907.
7. *Nashville (TN) Banner*, July 31, 1907.
8. *Bristol (VA) Herald Courier*, July 26, 1907.
9. *Chattanooga (TN) Daily Times*, July 31, 1907.
10. *Tazewell Republican*, July 25, 1907.
11. *Journal and Tribune*, July 27, 1907.
12. *Tazewell Republican*, July 25, 1907.
13. *Bristol Herald Courier*, July 24, 1907.
14. Ibid., July 26, 1907.
15. Ibid.
16. *Chattanooga News*, July 27, 1907.
17. *Bristol Herald Courier*, July 31, 1907.
18. *Journal and Tribune*, August 10, 1907.
19. *Nashville Banner*, July 31, 1907.
20. *Journal and Tribune*, August 10, 1907.

2. RMS *Lusitania*

21. *Clinch Valley News*, January 4, 1907.
22. *Tazewell Republican*, July 30, 1908.
23. *Clinch Valley News* (Bristol, VA), July 31, 1908.
24. *Tazewell Republican*, August 6, 1908.
25. Ibid., September 17, 1908.
26. Ibid., October 1, 1908.
27. Ibid., October 22, 1908.
28. Ellis Island Passenger Records, October 25, 1908.
29. *Tazewell Republican*, November 15, 1908.
30. *Roanoke (VA) Times*, March 17, 1910.
31. *Clinch Valley News*, May 14, 1915.
32. *Evening News* (Roanoke, VA), March 18, 1911.
33. *The World-News* (Roanoke, VA), October 13, 1913.
34. *Salem (VA) Times-Register and Sentinel*, August 12, 1915.
35. *The World-News*, August 24, 1914.
36. Ibid., September 30, 1914.
37. *Big Stone Gap (VA) Post*, July 3, 1918.
38. *Clinch Valley News*, July 26, 1918.

3. RMS *Titanic*

39. *Rockbridge County (VA) News*, April 25, 1912.
40. *Lexington (VA) Gazette*, April 18, 1902.
41. *Richmond (VA) Dispatch*, June 19, 1902.
42. *Roanoke Times*, May 16, 1909.
43. *Fairmont West Virginian*, February 9, 1912.
44. This biography of Robert Williams Daniel was originally published as "Banking on Survival: The Life of a Virginia *Titanic* Survivor" in *Voyage* 106, Official Journal of Titanic International Society, Inc., Winter 2018.
45. *Bedford (VA) Bulletin*, April 25, 1912.
46. *Rockbridge County News*, April 18, 1912.
47. Chirnside, *"Big Four" of the White Star Flee*.
48. *Bedford Bulletin*, April 25, 1912.
49. Chirnside, *"Big Four" of the White Star Fleet*.
50. Ibid.
51. Ellis Island Passenger Records, June 29, 1912.

52. *Tazewell Republican*, May 16, 1912.
53. *Big Stone Gap Post*, August 7, 1912.
54. *Salem Times-Register and Sentinel*, August 27, 1914.
55. Ibid., February 26, 1914.

4. USS *Mount Vernon*

56. *Clinch Valley News*, May 10, 1907.
57. Ibid., June 14, 1912.
58. Ibid., June 18, 1915.
59. Ibid., November 5, 1915.
60. Ibid., November 30, 1917.
61. Ibid., September 13, 1918.
62. Ibid., October 11, 1918.
63. Ibid.
64. Ibid.
65. Doyle, *History of the U.S.S.* Mount Vernon.
66. *Clinch Valley News*, January 24, 1919.
67. Ibid., December 22, 1922.
68. Ibid., October 4, 1918.

5. SS *Vestris*

69. Various sources have listed the number of victims as anywhere from 110 to 115. However, in counting each name of those lost, the total comes to 117, including the two deportees lost in the sinking.
70. Diana Powell, "Rev. Ernest Alonzo Jackson," Rambling Roots, http:// www.ramblingroots.com.
71. *News Leader* (Staunton, VA) May 9, 1903.
72. Powell, "Rev. Ernest Alonzo Jackson."
73. Passport application for Ernest Alonzo Jackson, August 14, 1923, National Archives and Records Administration.
74. *Knoxville (TN) News-Sentinel*, November 14, 1928.
75. Olivier, *Last Dance of the* Vestris.
76. *Bristol Herald Courier*, November 17, 1928.
77. Ibid.
78. *Knoxville (TN) Journal*, November 17, 1928.

79. *Bristol Herald Courier*, December 10, 1928.

80. Ibid.

81. Ibid.

82. Diana Powell, "Jacksons Plus Relatives and Neighbors," Rambling Roots, http://wc.rootsweb.ancestry.com.

83. *Times Dispatch* (Richmond, VA), June 17, 1906.

84. Information provided by Marc Brodsky, Public Services and Reference Archivist, Newman Library, Virginia Tech.

85. World War I Draft Registration, Charles Ingles Wade Stone, September 12, 1918.

86. *Princeton (IN) Daily Clarion*, November 26, 1928.

87. Ibid.

88. *Bristol Herald Courier*, November 14, 1928.

89. Information provided by Marc Brodsky, Public Services and Reference Archivist, Newman Library, Virginia Tech.

90. *Daily News* (New York, NY), November 6, 1938.

6. SS *Morro Castle*

91. Various totals for the number of victims have been put forth in different sources. However, according to longtime *Morro Castle* researcher Jim Kalafus, the correct number of lost is 128.

92. *Evening Star* (Washington, DC), September 15, 1934.

93. Oral history recounted by Sandra Holt, June 16, 2022.

94. World War I Draft Registration, Harry Acree Lipscomb, September 9, 1918.

95. Oral history recounted by Sandra Holt, June 16, 2022.

96. *Evening Star*, September 15, 1934.

97. Alexandria Police Foundation, Profiles of Courage: "Private Whitfield W. Lipscombe, 1930," http://www.alexandriapolicefoundation.org/memorial/profiles-of-courage/whitfield-lipscombe.htm.

98. Information written by and courtesy of Jim Kalafus.

99. Ibid.

100. *Central New Jersey Home News* (New Brunswick, NJ), September 16, 1934.

101. *Boston Globe*, September 15, 1934.

102. Burial records for the Lipscomb family provided by Spring Hill Cemetery, Lynchburg, Virginia.

103. Oral history recounted by Sandra Holt, June 16, 2022.

104. "*Morro Castle*: The Forgotten Voices," by Jim Kalafus, Gare Maritime, https://www.garemaritime.com/morro-castle-forgotten-voices/.
105. Oral history recounted by Sandra Holt, June 16, 2022.

7. Pearl Harbor

106. Certificate of Birth, Commonwealth of Virginia, Bureau of Vital Statistics, State Board of Health, James William Holzhauer, November 5, 1918.
107. *Bristol Herald Courier*, December 7, 1957.
108. Biographical and service documentation provided by Sam Crimm II.
109. Ibid.
110. "Body of McMinnville Man Who Died at Pearl Harbor During Japanese Attack Returned Home, to Be Buried Saturday," Thunder 1320, October 23, 2020, https://www.thunder1320.com.
111. Information provided through the research of the USS *Arizona* Mall Memorial Project at the University of Arizona.

8. USS *Perch*

112. *Evening Star*, April 11, 1942.
113. Ibid.
114. "On Eternal Patrol—The Discovery of USS *Perch* (SS-176)," On Eternal Patrol, http://www.oneternalpatrol.com.
115. "On Eternal Patrol—Lost Submarines of the U.S. Navy: David Albert Hurt, Sr.," On Eternal Patrol, http://www.oneternalpatrol.com.
116. *Evening Star*, November 22, 1945.
117. "On Eternal Patrol—USS *Perch* (SS-176)," On Eternal Patrol, http://www.oneternalpatrol.com.
118. Biographical and service information provided by Marian Brune McCreary.
119. Ibid.
120. *Cincinnati Enquirer*, January 2, 1946.
121. *Lebanon (VA) News*, November 30, 1945.
122. *Evening Star*, November 22, 1945.

9. Doughboys and GIs

123. *Richmond (VA) Times-Dispatch*, April 15, 1918.

124. *Richmond Times-Dispatch*, May 31, 1918.

125. *Rockbridge County News*, August 29, 1940.

126. *Bluefield (WV) Daily Telegraph*, January 7, 1945.

127. *Middlesboro (KY) Daily News*, March 23, 1945.

128. *Times-Dispatch*, February 27, 1945.

129. Biography written by and courtesy of Katy Jo Arrington Powers.

130. Oral history provided by Stuart Richardson, May 11, 2022.

10. Various Stories

131. *Big Stone Gap Post*, September 19, 1890.

132. *Salem Times-Register*, November 13, 1903.

133. *Big Stone Gap Post*, October 13, 1904.

134. *Bedford Bulletin*, February 21, 1907.

135. *Richmond (VA) Evening Journal*, May 28, 1910.

136. Ibid.

137. *Salem Times-Register and Sentinel*, June 29, 1911.

138. *Bedford Bulletin*, July 6, 1911.

139. *Tazewell Republican*, June 20, 1912.

140. *Clinch Valley News*, June 23, 1916.

141. Ibid., April 15, 1922.

142. *Crawford's Weekly* (Norton, VA), November 15, 1924.

143. *World News*, August 8, 1921.

144. *Lebanon News*, September 4, 1952.

145. *Rockbridge County News*, August 2, 1956.

146. *Rockbridge County News*, June 3, 1954.

147. *Buena Vista News* (Lexington, VA), August 9, 1956.

148. *Bedford Bulletin*, August 2, 1956.

149. *Lebanon News*, March 14, 1957.

BIBLIOGRAPHY

Bäbler, Günter. *Guide to the Crew of* Titanic: *The Structure of Working Aboard the Legendary Liner*. Stroud: The History Press, 2017.

Bailey, Thomas A., and Paul B. Ryan. *The* Lusitania *Disaster: An Episode in Modern Warfare and Diplomacy*. New York: The Free Press, 1975.

Behe, George. Titanic: *Safety, Speed and Sacrifice*. Illinois: Transportation Trails, 1997.

Burton, Hal. *The* Morro Castle: *Tragedy at Sea*. New York: The Viking Press, 1973.

Chirnside, Mark. *The 'Big Four' of the White Star Fleet: Celtic, Baltic & Adriatic*. Stroud: The History Press, 2018.

———. *The 'Olympic' Class Ships: Olympic, Titanic, Britannic*. Stroud: The History Press, 2011.

———. *RMS* Olympic: Titanic's *Sister*. Stroud: Tempus Publishing Limited, 2005.

Coyle, Gretchen F., and Deborah C. Whitcraft. *Inferno at Sea: Stories of Death and Survival Aboard the* Morro Castle. New Jersey: Down the Shore Publishing, 2014.

Doyle, Lieutenant-Commander James Madison. *A History of the U.S.S.* Mount Vernon. New York: Brooklyn Daily Eagle Job Department, 1919.

Drury, Bob and Tom Clavin. *Halsey's Typhoon: The True Story of a Fighting Admiral, an Epic Storm, and an Untold Rescue*. New York: Atlantic Monthly Press, 2007.

Fitch, Tad, and Michael Poirier. *Into the Danger Zone: Sea Crossings of the First World War*. Stroud: The History Press, 2014.

Fitch, Tad, J. Kent Layton and Bill Wormstedt. *On a Sea of Glass: The Life & Loss of the RMS* Titanic. Stroud: Amberley Publishing, 2015.

Gallagher, Thomas. *Fire at Sea: The Mysterious Tragedy of the* Morro Castle. Connecticut: The Lyons Press, 2003.

Geller, Judith B. Titanic: *Women and Children First*. New York: W.W. Norton, 1998.

Gleason, David King. *Virginia Plantation Homes*. Louisiana: Louisiana State University Press, 1989.

Goss, Michael, and George Behe. *Lost at Sea: Ghost Ships and Other Mysteries*. New Jersey: Galahad Books, 2005.

Hoehling, Adolph A. *They Sailed into Oblivion*. New York: Ace Books, 1959.

Hoehling, Adolph A., and Mary Hoehling. *The Last Voyage of the* Lusitania. New York: Henry Holt and Company, 1956.

King, Greg, and Penny Wilson. Lusitania: *Triumph, Tragedy, and the End of the Edwardian Age*. New York: St. Martin's Press, 2015.

Larson, Erik. *Dead Wake: The Last Crossing of the* Lusitania. New York: Crown Publishers, 2015.

Layton, J. Kent. Lusitania: *An Illustrated Biography of the Ship of Splendor*. Self-published, Lulu Press, 2007.

Lord, Walter. *Day of Infamy*. New York: Henry Holt and Company, 1957.

Maxtone-Graham, John. *The Only Way to Cross*. New York: Macmillan, 1978.

Olivier, Clint. *Last Dance of the* Vestris. Self-published, CreateSpace, 2013.

Sauder, Eric. *RMS* Lusitania: *The Ship & Her Record*. Stroud: Tempus Publishing Limited, 2005.

INDEX

ABOUT THE AUTHOR

Brandon Whited is a writer/historian who has spent his entire life in Southwest Virginia. Having first become fascinated with the *Titanic* and maritime history as a child, Brandon has served as a trustee with the Titanic International Society since 2019. He has had numerous articles and book reviews published in the society's quarterly journal, *Voyage*, and he is the author of *Gilded Tragedy: West Virginia's* Titanic *Widow*, a full-length biography of *Titanic* survivor Eloise Hughes Smith.

Drawing on his years of experience working in healthcare, Brandon was chosen to be one of the coauthors of the 2020 study *From the Front Lines of the Appalachian Addiction Crisis: Healthcare Providers Discuss Opioids, Meth and Recovery*. In 2021, he provided information and input for Greg King and Penny Wilson's *Nothing but the Night: Leopold & Loeb and the Truth behind the Murder That Rocked 1920s America*. In addition to his nonfiction works, Brandon has had a number of short stories, as well as some poetry, published in various literary journals dating back to 2005.